For
Nivi, Aka and Pavia,
who also want to experience
the wildlife of Greenland.

KJELD HANSEN

A FAREWELL TO GREENLAND'S WILDLIFE

Translated by Robin Worrall

COPENHAGEN 2002

Originally published in Denmark 2001
by Gads Forlag.
A Farewell to Greenland's Wildlife
Copyright © 2002 by Kjeld Hansen

Translated by Robin Worrall

Photographs: Euronatur (p. 12, 110, 128, cover), John Frikke (p. 62), Frank Wille (p. 30
Picture editing: Lars Gundersen
Maps p. 17, 61, 85: Kent Pørksen, Geographical Institute
Layout: Gads Forlag and Narayana Press, Gylling
Cover design: Harvey Macauley, Imperiet
Prepress and printing: Narayana Press, Gylling
Bound by J.P. Damm and Son, Randers

This book is set in Adobe Garamond

ISBN 87-89723-01-5

First Edition 2002

Kjeld Hansen, born 1947, educated at the Danish Journalist College. Has since 1983 been a freelance journalist and author specializing in environmental and consumer issues. Has travelled extensively world-wide reporting on environmental and wildlife conditions.

Danish author of the best-sellers "The Green Consumer Guide" (1990) and "Manual 2000" (2000) and also author of a series of books on sustainable lifestyles, green consumerism, etc. Has further written numerous articles and educational books on the greenhouse effect, wildlife conservation, sustainable development, East European environmental problems, environment and wildlife in Norway, Iceland and Greenland, etc. Extensive lecturing activities. Read more on website: www.greenland-wildlife.com

The author can be contacted via e-mail: gyldengroen@bog.dk or by phone: +45 56 52 22 70.

This edition has been produced by BæreDygtighed, Taastrupvej 31, DK-4672 Klippinge, Denmark in cooperation with Gads Forlag, Klosterstræde 9, DK-1157 Copenhagen K, Denmark.

Contents

Qaanaaq
Thule

Avanersuaq

Melville
Bay

The North
and Northeast
Greenland
National Park

Upernavik

Illoqqortoormiut
Scoresbysund

Uummannaq

Disko

Ilulissat
Jakobshavn

Qeqertarsuaq
Godhavn

Disko Bugt

Aasiaat
Egedesminde

Qasigiannguit
Christianshåb

Kangaatsiaq

Sisimiut
Holsteinsborg

Maniitsoq
Sukkertoppen

Tasiilaq
Ammassalik

Nuuk
Godthåb

Paamiut
Frederikshåb

Narsaq

Ivittuut

Qaqortoq
Julianehåb

Nanortalik

0   250   500

kilometers

Preface

To the bitter end

'All the Thick-billed Murres [Brünnich's Guillemot], Razorbills, Common and King Eider Ducks, and most of the Black-legged Kittiwakes were gone. Nesting cliffs where Bertelsen had recorded 500,000 murres and 100,000 kittiwakes were vacant of all bird life. The cliffs were still stained from seabird excrement, and ancient grass-covered kittiwake nests remained, but otherwise there was no sign of the thousands of birds that once flourished there.'

So wrote the American biologist Kurt K. Burnham when describing what he had observed sailing through the Uummannaq area in the summer of 2000.

Sailing by boat from Kangerlussuaq/Søndre Strømfjord to Qaanaaq/Thule, Burnham and three colleagues decided to take a closer look at the immensely rich bird life, which had been meticulously recorded 100 years earlier by Alfred Bertelsen, a Danish doctor*.

After eighteen days investigating two hundred and seven of the two hundred and ten bird sites identified by Bertelsen, the four Americans were shocked – everything was gone! Shot to oblivion.

Unfortunately, despite the Americans' disturbing revelations, the over exploitation of living resources in Greenland is old news – with destruction not simply confined to the Uummannaq area.

Alarm bells have rung since the late 1960s. Increasingly, though to little avail, biologists and scientists from Denmark, UK, Canada and many other countries have voiced their concerns about the over exploitation of wildlife in Greenland. Both the Danish Colonial Government of the day, and Greenlanders themselves have consistently and stubbornly turned a blind eye.

In today's modern Greenland hunting, fishing and trapping is taking place in a way that is ecologically and economically unsustainable. The unchecked use of living resources is taking place as if the present generation of Greenlanders were the last inhabitants on planet earth.

Brünnich's Guillemot, Beluga (White Whale), Common Eider, Walrus, Harbour Seal, King Eider, Artic Tern, Atlantic Halibut, Cod, Atlantic Salmon, Scallop – each species is a testimony to the tragic story and the consequences of decades of blind exploitation of living resources.

And this destruction of the biodiversity in Greenland appears likely to continue to the bitter end. Fishermen and hunters deny that a problem exists, and only a handful of politicians seem to have the courage to take the necessary action.

The alarming and most likely outcome is that present catch volumes will lead to even more drastic reductions in stocks, rendering them uneconomic in terms of their contribution to Greenland society. Some species will undoubtedly become extinct.

Additionally, there are intangible losses: Culture, identity and respect from the outside world. Future generations of young Greenlanders will never be able to experience the abundantly rich wildlife that Greenland once offered. Moreover, their fathers will be remembered worldwide as men that squandered everything away. An ancient proud hunting society will be reduced to a bitter shadowland of denial and repression.

The aim of this little book is to document the over exploitation of Greenland's unique fauna. Supported by factual evidence from Greenland's own biologists, the book illustrates the already comprehensive destruction. It demonstrates that Greenlanders are not living sustainably – and, seen from a modern perspective, shows that they never have.

If one were to project this negative development a mere 10–20 years into the future then the fate of most animals targeted for hunting will be sealed. As a result, wavering decision makers need to address this issue as a matter of urgency. This book attempts to outline the options available.

What may appear to be a regional problem is of global interest. Greenland's wildlife is part of humanity's common heritage and, increasingly, the eyes of the world will be focused on the way Greenlanders manage these living resources. If this book can make a contribution to helping the process start speeding up a little, then it will not have been written in vain.

Finally, I would like to thank the many people in Greenland, Canada, Iceland and Denmark who unselfishly provided information, comments and corrections. Without their encouragement and assistance none of this would have been possible.

Klippinge, Denmark, January 2002
Kjeld Hansen

---

* Alfred Bertelsen was a Danish doctor with an interest in ornithology. He practised and lived in Uummannnaq from 1905–1920 and collected information during his travels through the Uummannaq district (70°03' to 72°03'N). For fifteen years Bertelsen documented the breeding grounds of many different species including 30 Gyrfalcon nesting sites, as well as the locations and population densities of seabirds, divers, gulls and other species. Bertelsen's research, including maps of the 210 locations, was published under the title *The Birds of Uummannaq District (Fuglene i Umánaq distrikt)*, in the Danish scientific journal, *Meddelelser om Grønland*, (62:2).

Paradise lost

How bad is it really?

'If we compare our bird populations with those in Denmark for example, then a trip by boat or on foot along the Danish coastline reveals a wealth of different birds. By comparison, in our country we can sail for hours without seeing any birds. Previously there were lots of birds here. These changes have occurred from 1974–75 up to the present time.'

Written contribution to the Greenland Home Rule Parliament 'Seminar on living resources', held in Nuuk/Godthåb 9–11 October 1998, by Angmalortoq Olsen, a pensioner from Sisimiut/Holsteinsborg.

There was a time when the majestic bird cliffs between Disko Bay and Upernavik further to the north were teeming with Brünnich's Guillemot. Year after year, under the midnight sun of the short arctic summers more than 500,000 of these Guillemots provided rich pickings for Greenland's hunters.

Today only a few thousand birds are left, huddled together on the steep cliff sides.

Sixteen of the forty Brünnich's Guillemot colonies in West Greenland are already presumed extinct – destroyed by illegal summer hunting and egg collecting. Winter hunting of Brünnich's Guillemot in Greenland is now also affecting colonies in other countries. In the autumn of 2000 Iceland placed the Brünnich's Guillemot on its Endangered Species list, in a direct reference to unregulated hunting in Greenland.

Belugas once schooled along the whole west coast of Greenland – from Qaqortoq/Julianehåb in the south to Avanersuaq/Thule in the north. In Nuuk/Godthåb, the capital of Denmark's Greenland colony, children chewed fresh Beluga blubber from whales flensed in the harbour.

At least 8,000 Belugas were killed in Nuuk/Godthåb between 1874 and 1922, though the likely total was probably far higher. Whatever the figure, the scale of kills was sufficient to exterminate local whale populations in the Nuuk/Godthåb Fjord.

Today, Belugas are seldom spotted south of Maniitsoq/Sukkertoppen.

For centuries the Beluga has been an important catch for Greenland's hunters, but today this is virtually at an end. The Beluga population has fallen dramatically since 1981 – from approximately 19,000 then, to just 7,000 today. Hunting is still unregulated, and if this is allowed to continue without quotas, Belugas will be exterminated on Greenland's west coast within twenty years.

There was a time when Common Eiders hatched their olive green eggs everywhere on the rocks nearby every settlement. Women and children could collect as many eggs and down as they wanted, and everything appeared to be in perfect balance. Around 1850, in West Greenland alone, the quantity of Eider down purchased indicates that at least 110,000 Eider pairs were breeding at that time.

Nothing remains today of these enormous former colonies. Eider nests are rarely seen, and are scattered here and there – and always far away from towns. The decline continues – especially in proximity to larger settlements. Wanton hunting and egg collecting are responsible.

Brünnich's Guillemots, Belugas and Eiders are only three examples. Each in their own way demonstrates the consequences of decades of reckless exploitation of Greenland's living resources. The same tragic story applies to Walruses, Harbour Seals, King Eiders, Arctic Terns, Atlantic Halibut, Atlantic Salmon, Cod, Scallop and other species.

Only spectacular mammals such as Caribou and Muskox, which are terrestrial and therefore easy to count – or important species with a high market value such as Deep Sea Shrimps – are managed in a way that possibly justifies the term *sustainable exploitation*. Characteristically, catches of these species are firmly regulated based on modern principles. Specified close seasons, quotas, licensing and detailed catch rules allow for stock conservation by controlling the annual exploitation.

But the general picture is one that shows a highly impoverished animal world, especially in South and West Greenland, where inhabitants are concentrated in major population centres. In these areas the bird cliffs are bare and countless Eider colonies lie deserted. At the same time Walruses and Harbour Seals have been shot to oblivion from their haul-out sites. Even the last colonies of small Artic Terns are systematically cleared of eggs year after year.

Current stock status of principal hunted animals in Greenland.

Birds		Terrestrial mammals	
Brünnich's Guillemot	↓	Caribou	↑
Common Eider	↓	Muskox	↑
King Eider	↓		
Arctic Tern	↓	*Shrimps, Crabs and Bivalves*	
Geese	↑	Deep Sea Shrimp	↑
		Scallop	↓
Marine mammals		Snow Crab	↓
Polar Bear	↓?		
Ringed Seal	→?	*Fish*	
Harbour Seal	↓	Atlantic Halibut	↓
Bearded Seal	→?	Cod	↓
Harp Seal	↑	Redfish	↓
Hooded Seal	↑	Atlantic Salmon	↓
Walrus	↓	Arctic Char	↓
Beluga	↓		
Narwhal	→?		
Minke Whale	→?		
Fin Whale	→?		

↑: numbers are on the increase, ↓: numbers are over exploited/diminishing →: stocks are estimated to be stable ?: insufficient information on stocks. This summary is based on comprehensive source material – see narrative on individual species in chapter 3.

Beneath the waves the situation looks no better. All the economically valuable stocks of fish are either overfished or completely destroyed. Halibut stocks had already folded 60–70 years ago, never to recover. In the mid-1970s Cod stocks collapsed and have not recovered. During the 1960s Salmon boom some Danish, Norwegian and Faroese fishermen became millionaires, but in just 10 years stocks were exhausted – with the majority of North American Salmon rivers laid waste as a result.

Foreign fishing skippers had plenty to answer for during this 10-year bonanza. The annual by-catch of 250,000–500,000 Brünnich's Guillemot, which drowned in the drifting Salmon nets in the Davis Strait, undoubtedly contributed to emptying the Brünnich's Guillemot colonies in Disko Bay and northwards.

Today all valuable fisheries are subject to quotas, but in many cases the size of the quota leads to exploitation that negatively affects stocks. Currently, the most glaring example of this is Crab fishing, where quotas are set so high that stocks are likely to be destroyed within the next 5 years.

Sustainable exploitation

Exploitation of these 'living resources' – a telling expression used to describe animals, birds and fish in Greenland – has been, and still is carried out on a scale that even threatens the biological diversity – or *biodiversity*. It is possible to claim that this biodiversity is already sharply reduced over large areas – for example in the Uummannaq municipality, all of Disko Bay, around Nuuk/Godthåb and in most of the Qaqortoq/Julianehåb municipality.

The terms biological diversity or *biodiversity* are used to describe wildlife health: How many different species are to be found both on land and sea, whether there are sufficient animals to sustain genetically healthy stocks, and the viability of different ecosystems.

The term *sustainable exploitation* is used to describe how one can utilise these living resources without negatively affecting biological

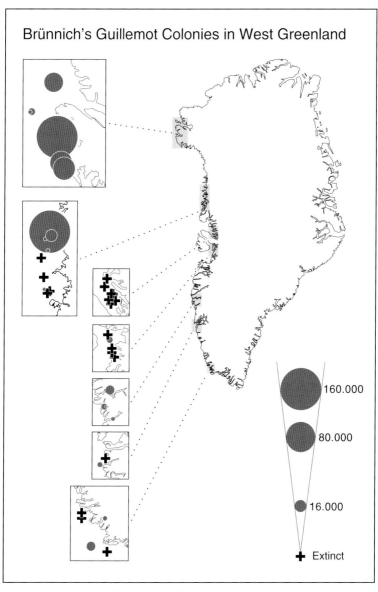

Brünnich's Guillemot Colonies in West Greenland

160.000

80.000

16.000

✚ Extinct

Today only a few small Brünnich's Guillemot colonies remain in central and south west Greenland, and many of the colonies are extinct. Source: *Topografisk Atlas Grønland, Copenhagen 2000.*

17

diversity. This entails that the exploitation of animal, bird and fish stocks, etc. is carried out in such a manner that also allows future generations to benefit from their use.

Consequently, it is not enough that animals are protected from certain extinction. Stocks also need to be large enough to allow people to exploit them in the future – both economically and for other purposes. For example cod, halibut and Salmon are still to be found around the coasts of Greenland but stocks are so over fished that present-day Greenlanders derive hardly any benefit from them.

The few exceptions

Apart from Deep Sea Shrimp fishing, Caribou and Muskox hunting, where strict quotas and controls apply, there are two exceptions to the general picture of over exploitation of living resources: Geese and seals (but not the Harbour Seal).

By all accounts, the six species of *geese* found in Greenland are thriving. There can be several good reasons why this is the case.

Three species occur exclusively in the North and Northeast Greenland National Park, protected by the vast distances. Possibly the greatest threat to these stocks is posed by helicopters engaged in raw materials exploration.

Two other species are found only sporadically and in limited numbers, whereas the remaining species, the White-fronted Goose, breeds along the populated west coast. In spite of this, numbers appear not to be affected by any appreciable hunting pressure, even though a brief hunting season has been permitted in the spring until very recently. This is probably because a tradition never developed for exploitation of White-fronted and the other species of geese. Undoubtedly, goose populations also benefit from vastly improved conditions in their wintering destinations in Europe and North America, where hunting bans, winter feeding and habitat protection have provided the birds with far better prospects for survival.

As far as *seal* numbers are concerned, Harp Seal populations have increased significantly, despite constant growth in kills over recent years. The latest scientific estimates indicate that the number of seal pups born on the Pack Ice off the coast of Newfoundland has increased from approx. 580,000 in 1990 to about 700,000 in 1994, which corresponds to a total population of nearly 5 million Harp Seals.

According to official statistics (*Piniarneq 2001*), Greenland's annual Harp Seal catch lies in the 56,660–82,491 range. This catch level clearly plays a minor role in comparison to the Canadian quotas, which are 3–5 times higher. In 1996 Canadians resumed commercial hunting in earnest with a quota of 275,000 Harp Seals allocated in both 1997 and 1998. According to the Canadian Government this catch level is viewed as sustainable with stocks expected to stabilise at around present numbers. The future will determine whether this prediction is correct.

Nevertheless a large question mark hangs over the Harp Seal catch in Greenland. Thousands of seal carcasses are dumped in the sea every year, as no possible uses for the considerable quantity of meat have been found. In Greenland alone, this catch amounts to a total weight of more than 5,700 tons (see p. 138).

The skins are sold but this is only possible due to artificially high prices maintained by subsidies running to millions. Nevertheless, the Greenland fur industry operates at a considerable loss, which is covered year after year by the Greenland Home Rule Government.

Since 1980 a large-scale subsidy culture has developed around the hunting business. Hunters are guaranteed minimum prices with skins bought and stockpiled, irrespective of the number of sealskins offered for sale. Additionally, there are numerous subsidies that include interest-free and repayment-free loans, interest subsidies and guarantees for the purchase of dinghies, outboard motors, hunting trips and equipment, and subsidised fuel benefits.

The subsidies for purchasing sealskins alone have increased from DKK 7.8 million in 1981 to DKK 44.4 million in 1999. For the 2001 financial year DKK 35 million has been earmarked to subsidise the purchase of sealskins.

In Spring 2001 KNAPK, the organisation representing fishermen and hunters, tabled their demands for guaranteed minimum prices of fish and shrimp. This development, if successfully pressed through, could quickly detonate a bomb under Greenland's whole economy.

The colonial legacy

Over exploitation of living resources in Greenland has been taking place for more than a hundred years. What present day Greenlanders and visiting tourists praise as a unique wildlife environment in a pristine arctic landscape, is today just a faint shadow of its original biological diversity.

It is worth noting that the original driving force behind this ruthless over exploitation was the Royal Greenland Trade Department (Den Kongelige Grønlandske Handel, commonly known as KGH), which was started in 1774 when trade in this arctic colony was taken over by the Kingdom of Denmark. For more than 200 years KGH supervised the commercial exploitation of these living resources. With the benefit of hindsight this was both a threat to Greenland's wildlife and to the very identity of Greenland itself.

However, the fact that the Greenland Home Rule Government took over responsibility from the Danish State in 1979 has made little difference. On the contrary it can almost be said that, to a considerable extent, Parliament and Government have continued to pursue the old KGH policy of maximum commercial exploitation. The over exploitation continues otherwise unabated, notwithstanding the fact that KGH has been transformed into companies such as Royal Greenland A/S, Great Greenland A/S and NuKa A/S, and that these companies are all owned by the Greenland Home Rule Government.

For example, while the Greenland Home Rule Parliament has had responsibility for managing stocks, the Beluga population has more than halved in the last 20 years. Commercial buying of up to 25,000 Brünnich's Guillemots annually is also sanctioned without much hesitation. As late as spring 2000 Parliament voted unanimously to allow commercial collection of gulls' eggs. This was voted through, despite clear warnings from amongst others the Greenland Institute of Natural Resources (*Pinngortitaleriffik*), which was concerned about increasing pressure on already severely thinned-out bird colonies, and on species other than gulls.

The Greenland Home Rule Government established the Greenland Institute of Natural Resources as recently as 1995. The Institute's main role is to advise Greenland's politicians on sustainable management of the living resources, but it is the politicians who have to make the necessary decisions – and they are hesitating.

In fear of hunters

Paradoxically enough, fishermen and hunters are the ones blocking the way forward to increasing sustainable living resources' management. Although animals, birds and fish are the bedrock of their existence, they obstinately reject any talk of regulating this exploitation. It seems this group is bent on sinking the boat on which they float.

Despite repeated warnings, both from former hunters, biologists and international scientific commissions, the Greenland Home Rule Parliament is reluctant to take action – because members are apprehensive as to the reaction of the 2,569 registered professional hunters and their family networks. This constitutes a powerful factor, which in the opinion of any Greenland politician has to be taken into consideration – if he wishes to retain his seat in the Parliament chamber in Nuuk.

Hunters are representative of Greenland's culture and original identity, so the population is broadly sympathetic to their cause, even though the hunting business is economically insignificant. Some would argue that this population group only enjoys an acceptable living standard by virtue of enormous subsidies, but also that they represent one of the few remaining elements of the original Greenland. If we have no hunters then we are nothing, it has been said.

Professional hunters know better and they trust neither Greenland Home Rule biologists nor politicians. Leif Fontain, a fisherman and hunter from Sisimiut/Holsteinsborg, is the chairman of KNAPK, the Organisation of Fishermen and Hunters in Greenland. In an article in the Greenland newspaper AG/Grønlandsposten on 9 January 2001 he described hunters' attitudes to biologists and politicians. His comments appeared in a long article entitled: 'Wildlife, management, sustainability, and neo-colonialism in Greenland'. Here are some excerpts:

'(…) History tells us that wildlife in our country has always been sought after. In the period after Greenland became a Danish colony a warlike situation existed with the colonial powers over the question of whaling. Even the Danish kings of the time did not hesitate to threaten inhabitants with extermination if they didn't catch more seals, so that he could earn more on seal blubber. Colonial powers needed more of the oil extracted from blubber to light their countries. Additionally, prospects of mineral riches have also always interested colonial powers.

In these modern decades, there are modern people in a modern (neo-colonial) society such as lawyers, economists, biologists, journalists and other well-meaning folks, who oppose the hunting of wild animals principally on the grounds of cruelty to animals, animal welfare and the danger of wild animal extinction.

By splitting the complete picture into separate components, for example the food chain in Greenland, biologists in the Greenland Institute of Natural Resources are arguing in favour of a peripheral case, which arouses fanatical concern in today's modern world – namely that unfortunate sweet animals should have the right to survive so that modern people and intelligent animals can be showcased side by side in perfect harmony.

It is worth noting that this publicity provides an excellent illustration of the extent to which Greenland's ecosystems are determined and prioritised by needs and pressures coming from the outside world. In this debate not a single fisherman or hunter's voice has been heard. There should be no mistaking the intentions. The surrounding world and modern democracies will once more instruct us what to do. I contend that this is simply just another example of modern colonialism. To a large extent, if our rulers give in to outside pressures and introduce sanctions along top-down management lines, it would be another example of post colonialism. (…)'

Wildlife conservation is lagging behind

Regulating the pressure of hunting is one way to safeguard biological diversity; protection of animals' habitats is another. By protecting their important breeding grounds and the locations where they congregate and feed animals will be safeguarded against hunting and catching. The safeguarding of habitats, where animals can breed in peace, also allows the possibility for hunting to continue.

In this field Greenland's wildlife management is lagging far behind. Actually, one of the *least* used laws in Greenland is the 1980 Parliament Law no. 11 concerning wildlife conservation. This law has been in the process of revision for years with 2002 as the year when the process may be completed.

True, 43 per cent of the total Greenland area is covered by a single conservation measure for the protection of the North and Northeast Greenland National Park, which is the world's largest conservation area. This preservation dates right back to 1974, when the Danish Parliament voted to protect this enormous area after recommendations by Greenland's Provincial Council. This area is invaluably important for such species as: Walrus, Polar Bear, Muskox, geese, waders and many other life forms.

But, in reality it is not in this uninhabited high-arctic zone where development of modern Greenland is excerting most pressure. On the contrary, the vast majority of people live in the low-arctic zone and this is where most of the pressure on wildlife is taking place today.

By contrast, wildlife protection is minimal in these populated areas. Outside the North and Northeast Greenland National Park's boundaries less than 3 per cent of Greenland is covered by preservation orders, and these also include marine areas.

For example, in 1998 it was in the low-arctic zone that the Greenland Home Rule Government gave German car manufacturer Volkswagen permission to build a 35-kilometre gravel road from Kangerlussuaq/Søndre Strømfjord into the inland ice – through a Caribou wilderness. Volkswagen will construct a further 100 kilometres of test tracks on the inland ice, together with a hotel and workshops, for testing new car models under extreme conditions. The German corporation has invested a three-figure million sum so far, but otherwise information about the test facility is very thin on the ground.

The go-ahead for the entire project was given in 1998 without any kind of environmental evaluation. With the exception of the German project's operators and the Greenland Home Rule Government, access to the site is strictly prohibited to all – including Greenlanders and everyone else for that matter.

There are a total of only seven large conservation areas in Greenland. The table below shows the distribution of land, sea and ice areas.

Location	Total area km²	Ice-free land km²	Sea areas km²	Ice km²
National Park	956,700	176,076	110,600	670,024
Melville Bay	7,957	703	5,193	2,061
Lyngmarken	2	2	0	0
Paradisdalen	90	90	0	0
Qinnguadalen	45	45	0	0
Akilia	1.4	1.4	0	0
Ikka Fjord	6	0	6	0
Total area protected	964,801	176,917	115,799	672,085

Conservation areas in Greenland as of 1 January 2001.

Hunting laws – what hunting laws?

Apart from the conservation areas mentioned above there are 12 birdlife sites that have access restrictions. These are spread along 2,200 kilometres of coast stretching from Qaanaaq/Thule in the north to Qaqortoq/Julianehåb in the south. These include specific cliffs and islands with breeding colonies of Guillemot, Common Eider and Arctic Tern. Landing at, or approaching the sites within 500 metres is forbidden in the period 1 May to 31 August. Nonetheless, most restrictions are openly flouted.

These regulations are only applied in a few municipalities. In Upernavik, for example, prohibited access signs have been put up at the four birdlife conservation sites, with access controlled by a gamekeeper. Regulations are infringed on a massive scale in other municipalities, for example at Saattuarsuit near Grønne Ejland and on the Ydre Kitsissut island group in southern Greenland.

A prime example of the consequences of this lack of respect for conservation laws can be found on the 1,070 metre-high Salleq bird cliff – the only protected location in the Uummannaq municipality. Salleq was once home to an enormous colony of Brünnich's Guillemot, numbering an estimated 150,000 individuals in 1949. Since 1989 the colony has been extinct – the result of illegal summer hunting and egg collection.

Regulations also preclude shooting and making unnecessary noise within 5 kilometres of all bird cliffs with their populations of Brünnich's Guillemot, Common Guillemot, Razorbill, Little Auk, Black-legged Kittiwake, Northern Fulmar, and Great Cormorant. The same regulations also apply for everyone within 200 metres of low islands with breeding populations of Common and King Eider, Black Guillemot, Arctic Tern and seagulls other than Kittiwake, but with the exception of egg collectors.

This is probably the most flouted regulation of the few official attempts made to protect birdlife during the breeding season. Over the past years (see p. 32 ff.) there are countless accounts, observations and sightings documented in several reports – amongst others from the Greenland Institute of Natural Resources, and in many newspaper articles – that confirm this lack of respect for the laws governing access and hunting restrictions shown by hunters, leisure hunters and others in Greenland. 'Hunting rules only apply within sight of a township', is the popular justification for this attitude.

Denmark's Nelsonian blind spot

Ultimately, 11 sites in Greenland totalling 15,458 km² have been categorised under the Ramsar Convention as Wetlands of International Importance.

The Convention on Wetlands, signed in Ramsar, Iran, in 1971, is an intergovernmental treaty which provides the framework for national action and international cooperation for the conservation and wise use of wetlands and their resources. There are presently 128 Contracting Parties to the Convention, with 1,095 wetland sites.

Only 28 of these lie within the artic climate zone: 5 in Spitsbergen, 7 in Siberia, 4 in Canada, 1 in Alaska and 11 in Greenland.

The sites in Greenland have to comply with the Convention's aims for their protection, and especially in relation to birdlife. Although the 11 sites were identified in 1987, they have never been legitimised under Greenland law. This has meant that hunting, trapping and access remain unregulated.

However, a small proportion of Greenland's Ramsar sites are protected by other legislation. Two areas, Hochstetter Forland and Kilen comprising a total of 2,961 km², are situated within the North and Northeast Greenland National Park and are thus covered by the special regulations applying there. But these regulations offer no protection against mineral and oil exploration and extraction. Additionally, hunters from Illoqqortoormiut/Scoresbysund are still allowed to hunt in the North and Northeast Greenland National Park for Polar Bear in the traditional way.

Three other areas are partially or completely protected by hunting laws covering breeding sanctuaries.

The non-implementation of the Ramsar Convention has had serious consequences. Two important wildlife areas, both included on the Ramsar list, have been denuded of their outstanding birdlife.

Uncontrolled hunting and fishing for Scallops has driven 30,000 King Eider out of the Aqajarua-Sullorsuaq area in Disko Bay. This happens to be Canada-Greenland's most important moulting site for the combined populations of King Eider in the western Arctic region. The Aqajarua-Sullorsuaq site comprises 224 km².

The other area is Grønne Ejland in Disko Bay, which was once home to the world's largest breeding colony of Arctic Tern, comprising between 80,000 and 100,000 breeding pairs. Unchecked egg collection, hunting and other disruptions have driven the birds away. The Grønne Ejland area covers 69 km².

This non-implementation over the past 14 years is a clear violation of the Ramsar Convention's rules. According to Nick Davidson, Deputy Secretary General, of the Ramsar Secretariat in Switzerland, implementation has to be carried out within six years of a site being designated.

In real terms the 11 Ramsar designated sites in Greenland, which officially comprise approximately 1.5 million hectares – an area twice the size of the Danish island of Zealand – have only existed in theory. No administrative plans, conservation rules, traffic regulations or other forms of legal protection have ever been drawn up in relation to the Convention's articles for the prevention of designated locations and their wildlife content.

Even though it is common knowledge that Greenland has never fulfilled the terms of the agreement, and that birdlife was known to have vanished in more locations, Denmark's National Forest and Nature Agency, as the designated Ramsar Administrative Authority, has turned a Nelsonian eye on the Convention's non-implementation.

According to Nick Davidson, the Danish National Forest and Nature Agency is the designated Ramsar Administrative Authority for Denmark and Greenland, and is responsible for reporting on progress and deterioration of the sites, including those in Greenland. Yet, despite this fact, the Ramsar Secretariat in Switzerland has never heard that there might be problems in Greenland.

But the National Forest and Nature Agency in Copenhagen denies ultimate responsibility. Jens Peter Simonsen, Deputy Director, confirms that Denmark is the signatory to the Ramsar Convention on behalf of Greenland, and that the National Forest and Nature Agency is the designated authority reporting on implementation status. But he passes the buck over to the Greenland Home Rule Government. Jens Peter Simonsen states that it is the Home Rule Government that is responsible for sites in Greenland, and that the National Forest and Nature Agency merely passes the information on without taking a position as to whether this tallies with the actual situation on the ground.

In June 1999 the Bureau of Minerals and Petroleum of the Greenland Home Rule Government issued a set of 'Rules for fieldwork and reporting regarding mineral resources (excluding hydrocarbons) in Greenland'. This publication identifies a considerable number of important wildlife sites. Because they host sizeable bird populations, all the non-implemented Ramsar sites are included on the list. However, despite being identified by the Bureau of Minerals and Petroleum none are covered by Greenland's legislation. There are restrictions, for example applying to helicopter flights and other traffic, for ensuring that wildlife is disturbed as little as possible in the designated areas. These rules only apply to the exploration for raw materials.

The rising tide of international criticism

While Beluga and Walrus populations disappear from the waters around Greenland, and the enormous bird colonies teeming with life fall silent, a new chorus of voices is making itself heard both in and outside Greenland. This criticism comes from organisations like NAMMCO, CAFF, ICES, JCCM, RAMSAR, CITES, WWF, DOF, BirdLife International and other environmental organisations, commissions and international partners.

Greenland is on the point of being identified as the Arctic's black sheep, or a Nordic equivalent to Malta – where anything that moves is shot.

'Friends' also raise their eyebrows. Canada has repeatedly voiced its criticism about the management of Common and King Eider, and is especially concerned about small whales. In autumn 2000 Iceland placed the Brünnich's Guillemot on its Endangered Species list in a direct reference to alleged over exploitation of Icelandic breeding birds at their wintering sites in Greenland.

Officially, up to now, Denmark has said very little, but behind the scenes the Ministry of Environment and Energy is increasingly alarmed. The reduction of wildlife in Greenland is viewed with concern. The Government and Danish Parliament will hardly be able to keep all this under wraps for much longer because Denmark is Greenland's principal sponsor in this skewed development via an annual block grant of DKK 2.8 billion. The paymaster is also responsible for how the money is used. In fact Danish taxpayers pay 80 per cent (1998) of the running costs of the Greenland Home Rule Government, equivalent to a subsidy of DKK 50,000 for every man, woman and child in Greenland.

But the most disturbing aspect for Greenland's society is the burgeoning international criticism. As the international community tunes in to what is happening in Greenland, critical media disclosures will arouse violent indignation. Only this time it is about much more than baby seals, Brigitte Bardot or Greenpeace. The myth of the sustainable Inuit is heading for a fall.

From Kayak to Yamaha

How has it come to this?

'The crazy persecution of this magnificent bird resulted in its astronomical number being sharply reduced over a period of time – something that was almost inconceivable given the numbers of these birds. Finally, after many and considerable obstacles were overcome, the birds were totally protected during the breeding season along the entire coastline.'

Knud Oldendow, on the Common Eider in *Greenland – the country and its people in our time* (Grønland – Folk og Land i vore Dage), 1936. Knud Oldendow was Chief Administrative Officer of south Greenland. Later he became section head in the Greenland Administration in Denmark.

This consistent over exploitation – representing more than a century of predatory extermination – is the real reason behind the loss of Greenland's magnificent wildlife over the years.

But, in terms of flesh and blood what do words like 'over exploitation' or 'ruthless exploitation' really mean?

The following passages provide a snapshot of what actually lies hidden behind the many abstract words and terms that can be read in a plethora of scientific reports on the need for 'sustainable exploitation' of living resources in Greenland. The accounts demonstrate that even well disciplined biologists can be shocked, when directly confronted with Greenland hunters' mindless treatment of the last remnants of biodiversity of former times.

In the summer of 1998 a biologist from the Greenland Institute of Natural Resources was engaged in fieldwork south of Upernavik. He described the observations that he had noted in his diary to the Greenland newspaper Sermitsiaq, 25 September, 1998. The title of the article read: *Just another ordinary day at the Kingittoq bird cliffs?*

The following passages represent a comprehensive extract:

Friday, 17 July, 1998. – We wake early, the sun is shining and temperatures in the tent have risen to undreamt levels. We are just south of Upernavik, west of Kingittoq, which is the largest of the four remaining Guillemot colonies in southern Upernavik. We are here, today and for the next 11 days, to carry out research on how Brünnich's Guillemots are doing. Since their introduction in 1989, have the tighter hunting regulations had a beneficial effect, or is the trend continuing in the direction of a drastic fall in population sizes, in the same way as the last 25 years?

Today the only thing we know for certain is that there are 10 fewer breeding birds to count than yesterday. The birds were shot late yesterday evening close to Kingittoq. We were somewhat outraged because the birds are supposedly protected by a conservation order at the present time. But, all things considered, it was only 10 Guillemots and Upernavik's inhabitants are only allowed to shoot Guillemots for just a short season – so who can blame them if they occasionally shoot a few Guillemots in the close season. (…)

Tuesday, 21 July. – (…) Today we can confirm that some of the Guillemots are bringing food back in their beaks – so eggs are beginning to hatch. Guillemot pairs will be busy in the coming 3–4 weeks, because every breeding pair now has an extra mouth to feed. For approximately 100 Guillemots this task will be impossible. These are the 100 Guillemots that lost their mates yesterday evening. Three boats were out shooting simultaneously and in less than two hours the damage was done! We feel frustrated on behalf of the Guillemots. The single parents remain looking after their eggs or chicks, waiting in vain to be relieved. At some point hunger will force them to abandon their offspring, imposing an immediate death sentence on the hatchlings in question. The egg or chick's temperature will quickly fall and it is only a matter of time before the embryo or chick dies or is taken by a Glaucous Gull. We are keeping our fingers crossed in the hope that yesterday evening's episode was an exception – actually number two. On our way back to camp we had to kill two Guillemots and two Black-legged Kittiwakes to put them out of their misery. They were perched huddled up on flat rocks at the base of the cliff – maimed but not dead.(…)

Friday, 24 July. – (…) There has been shooting again this evening near Kingittoq – 40 shots were fired close to Kingittoq in a 35-minute burst with 26 Guillemots killed. However, 6 of those were shot for no particular reason and were simply left to float in the water, dead or half-dead. These incidents are beginning to seem preposterous to us. It is bad enough that these people apparently have no intention of complying with hunting regulations, shooting breeding birds and in the process sentencing not only this year's offspring to death, but also their offspring for the next 10, 15 or 20 years to come. But furthermore, if they do not even respect the spoils they shoot, not bothering to retrieve them then, yes, something is drastically wrong.

Saturday, 25 July. – (…) Unfortunately our work was interrupted. Some of the birds have been frightened off the cliff by volleys of shots. Also, it is the same two boats that we saw operating together five days ago. Having discovered our presence near the cliff, the shooting stops for a while and the hunters appear obviously somewhat bewildered. We headed for camp and had hardly tied up our rubber dinghy before the shooting started again – this time 26 shots and 13 hits. That evening a new boat, obviously sailing through, arrived in the area and promptly dispatched 6 Guillemots with 26 shots. We begin to realise that these events we are witnessing are not uncommon – just a thoroughly ordinary occupation on a completely ordinary day at Kingittoq.

Sunday, 26 July. – A thick fog hangs cold and damp like a heavy shroud over the camp near Kingittoq. Not one bird cliff is visible. We chat about this and that and try to ignore the somewhat depressive mood that often accompanies this type of weather. A positive benefit of the fog is that the Guillemots can be at peace for a while.

However, this illusion is shattered in the afternoon. First 70 shots ring out, then 13 more. Later still, with visibility down to 2–300 metres, shots really start in earnest. Bullets are whizzing everywhere and we are forced to intervene with a VHF call to the boat. Our call-up is met with silence, but the firing stops abruptly. We crawl back into our sleeping bags and try to forget another … day near Kingittoq.

Monday, 27 July. – Our last day. We are busy packing up camp. The Guillemot study has gone well and we can now go home and complete the work. Provisional results indicate that Guillemot numbers in Upernavik's southern colonies have declined sharply. Exactly by how much will only become apparent when we factor in data on natural variation. A continued decline is expected. During the time we were here, 3–4 per cent of the breeding population was shot with 4–5 per cent of offspring lost as a result of this hunting.(…)

Finally, we finished packing up and, with the boat loaded, we are on the point of casting off, when we hear a dinghy on the other side of the fiord. Its owner is in the process of bagging a couple of Guillemots – while they are still around. I wonder whether the expedition's final day might really be the last thoroughly ordinary day I will experience near Kingittoq?'

Dreams of arctic paradise

The biologist's account of his experiences at Kingittoq finds endless repetition in countless different ways along the length and breadth of Greenland's rocky coastline. Eye-witnesses' accounts make for salutary reading: Hunters pumping gun shots into huge whales with no earthly hope of killing them, hunters cruising around in motorboats shooting down seagulls without bothering to stop and collect the kill, and even hunters killing walruses merely for the tusks' sake, and then allowing the carcasses to rot.

Scientific reports over the last fifty years have accumulated in stacks, metres thick, all reaching the same conclusion: Wildlife in Greenland is disappearing to the point of extinction.

The determining factor is quite simply Greenlanders' unwillingness, or inability to regulate catches at a sustainable level.

Very few people outside Greenland have heard about the enormous abuse of this vast country's living resources. In a world where most peoples' images are limited to media coverage of Frederik, crown prince of Denmark, sledging through magnificent uninhabited East Greenland with the Sirius patrol in the year of 2000, it is hard to believe that this dazzling-picture-postcard landscape represents only one side of reality.

And when facts threaten to change our dream image we mobilise the additional force of psychological aversion. There is no doubt that idealised representations of an unspoilt Greenlandic paradise are deeply entrenched in the hearts of most people. Even experienced parliamentarians, professional journalists, and scientifically trained men and women appear to avert their gaze when the unpleasant aspects of Greenland society sail into view.

The man in a kayak with raised harpoon, the camouflaged hunter, inching across the ice, the woman flensing a seal on the beach holding the traditional ulo – we all have our own image of a Greenland Inuk in our minds' eye. Yet we continue to cling to these traditional images of Greenlanders despite the advent of Yamaha engines, fibreglass dinghies, Remington rifles, snow-scooters, GPS navigators, helicopters and Tenson clothing.

We seem to want to keep this dream of an unspoilt Greenland alive in our hearts. This explains why so many of us simply close our eyes to the depressing sides of Greenland society: The terrible social problems, the deficient democracy, and wholesale destruction of living resources.

Many of Greenland's politicians, trade unionists, business leaders and intellectuals still willingly play a role that fits into the picture-postcard image of this unspoilt virgin land, way up north. But they may be doing more damage than good to their country? Problems do not disappear simply by a process of collective denial. Or, put another way: The numbers of Beluga, Walrus, Greenland Halibut, Scallop, Eider and Brünnich's Guillemot will not increase by merely arguing that biologists have got it wrong.

In addition there are demographic and technological changes that have affected Greenland society over the last 100 years. These also exert a pull in the wrong direction in relation to Greenland's old hunting society. But all modern societies have been subjected to these developments and most countries have managed the process of change without squandering all their living resources.

Today's Greenland *is* a modern society, which unhesitatingly takes advantage of the latest technology: For example, 35 per cent of all homes in Greenland boast a PC. But, the management of living resources still occurs as if Greenland hunters were paddling their kayaks, and using harpoons and bird arrows as in the days of yore, when wildlife resources seemed inexhaustible and the population was far smaller than now.

The population explosion

Greenland's population in the twentieth century increased more than four-fold. Around 1900 there were just 11,621 Greenlanders, but their numbers have grown to 49,369 by 2000. The greatest growth occurred in a ten-year period from 1960–1970, when the population increased by approx. 8,000.

Today, in line with other modern societies annual growth is modest, at less than 1 per cent.

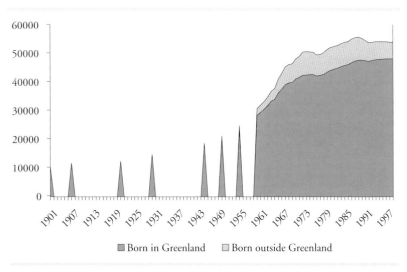

Population of Greenland 1901–2000. Source: *Statistics Greenland.*

Problems particularly exist on the west coast. These are closely connected to the fact that this is where the population – and much of the living resources – is concentrated. Of the 49,369 people making up the Greenland population (2000) only 6.6 per cent, or 3,258 inhabitants, live in East Greenland's two municipalities.

Greenland's 17 towns are currently home to 81.5 per cent of the population, while 16.5 per cent live in 59 settlements. The remaining 2 per cent live on sheep farms, or at fishery and hunting stations. Over the last 30–40 years the population has been concentrated in towns. This is an ongoing trend.

The Nuuk/Godthåb area is the biggest magnet. In 2000, a quarter of the population (24.6 per cent) lived in the capital. Ten years earlier the corresponding figure was 22.8 per cent.

Growth of population in towns: Number of inhabitants (born in Greenland) in the Nuuk/Godthåb municipality area, 1970–2000.

1970	1980	1990	2000
5,563	6,730	8,558	10,625*

* Add 3,213 persons born outside Greenland to this figure.

Population leaving settlements: Number of inhabitants in the Qassimi-ut settlement, Qaqortoq/Julianehåb municipality area, 1970–2000.

1970	1980	1990	2000
185	141	98	62

Source: *Statistics Greenland.*

On the face of it, although mistakenly, one might be led to believe that concentrating the population in just a few towns would be advantageous for animals and birdlife, simply because the abandonment of dwellings and settlements would result in a greater number of uninhabited areas.

This has not happened, mainly for two reasons.

Firstly, towns have many more consumer durables on offer. The hunter and his family naturally want to have their share of these items. To satisfy this need today's hunting income has to be on a far larger scale in comparison to the times when hunting culture was purely a question of survival for those living in remote areas. This is why hunting trips are more frequent and – as living resources diminish – they last longer.

Secondly, mobility has played a decisive role. Assisted by motorboats, snow-scooters and modern telecommunications the limitations once imposed on hunters by kayak, umiak and dog sledge, vanished long ago. Other developments include commercial buying of kills – Beluga and Brünnich's Guillemot for example – by trading vessels and shore facilities. This also increases the pressure on living resources.

Kayaks in museums of the imagination

Although far too often forgotten the winds of change have been blowing through Greenland's hunting culture for more than half a century. Just read the 1952–53 yearbook published by the Danish Tourist Association, which chose to bring Denmark's northern colony under the spotlight that year. Writing about jobs and occupations in Greenland under the heading 'From kayak to cutter' (remember the year was 1952), the book's editor, Kjeld Rask Therkildsen noted:

'(…) Although it is an increasingly rare occurrence, even today some Greenlanders still set out in their fragile, graceful kayaks to gather food for the family. Where previously hunters glided silently forward between rocks and ice floes with bird arrows and harpoons at the ready, now fishermen set their nets and lines to the throbbing sound of motor and fishing boats' engines reverberating round the grey cliff walls (…).'

In just 60 years, the number of motorboats in Greenland has risen 20-fold. Simultaneously, and particularly since 1960, better and more powerful engines have arrived on the market – above all outboard motors. Consequently today, any professional or leisure hunter with a fast speedboat can cover in a couple of hours the same distance that previously took his father several days to complete.

This means that the very smallest corners of West Greenland's deep fiords are accessible. Even remote islets out in the skerries – places that would otherwise never be visited – are exploited today. Despite their remoteness from human habitation, no trout stream, Eider colony, White-tailed Eagle eyrie or bird cliff is free from predators. Along that part of Greenland's coastline stretching from Nanortalik in the south right up to a couple of hundred kilometres north of Upernavik – i.e. along the entire southern and western coastline – the

0   250   500
kilometers

The use of modern motorboats has led to a dramatic increase in the range covered by west Greenland hunters. Using a speedboat fitted with an 85 HP outboard engine just about every ice-free area along the west coast of Greenland can be reached from a town or settlement within three hours. The large circles indicate the range from towns (3 hours sailing time at 20 knots). The small circles indicate the range from settlements (3 hours sailing time at 10 knots). Source: Technical report no. 20, 1998, Greenland Institute of Natural Resources.

hunting area of one town or settlement starts where another's ends. Stretching for more than 1,800 kilometres, this coastline today forms one unbroken hunting ground, through which an armada of motorboats sails daily.

A vast hunting ground

A 1989 census of motorboats in the Upernavik municipality – where at that time 2,361 people lived – counted 407 motorboats, mostly powered by outboard engines. This corresponded to one motorboat for every 5–6 inhabitants.

Number of motorboats in Greenland, 1939–1999.

1939	1949	1999
73	288	1.469

Source: *Wildlife protection in Greenland. Technical report no. 29, 2000, Greenland Institute of Natural Resources.*

In recent times many more Greenlanders have become interested in building cabins in the open countryside, mainly up the fiords. These are basically small buildings (30–50 m^2), used very much like summerhouses in Denmark. During the holidays and at weekends, people sail by boat to their cabins, where they relax with a bit of fishing and hunting.

Littering an open landscape with cabins is not the problem. For example, even though there are hundreds of them along the Nuuk/Godthåb fiord they are hardly visible in the huge landscape. The biggest problem is that they actually contribute to increasing the range covered by hunting and fishing activities. Amongst other things many local stocks of Arctic Char have been severely affected.

Swarms of pleasure boats and part-time hunters around the larger towns and settlements force professional hunters to operate even further afield. This means that hunters also visit remote, previously undisturbed areas more frequently.

Modern times

Without a shadow of doubt many fishermen and hunters have understood the consequences of the dramatic increase in hunting pressure – but most keep their mouths shut.

After all, it is also difficult to advocate restricting one's own occupation – especially when having to provide a family with food, a centrally heated house with mains electricity, telephone, TV and running water as well. Then there are overheads to cover: The cost of fishing tackle, dinghy, outboard engine, various firearms, ammunition and fuel, not to mention the cash required for the purchase of smart clothes for the kids, video films, modern furniture and if possible a winter holiday somewhere south.

Hunters are no exception: Lots of bills need paying every month, and increasing numbers of Belugas will need to be sold to keep up families' living standards. Wildlife pays a terrible price, because a professional hunter returning to port every other day with a haul of possibly 50 Guillemots will be lucky to get DKK 1,000 for his efforts.

Previously, hunters only needed to hunt for food, clothes and the few other essential items needed for life on the settlement. But now hunters need to earn money to buy some of those tempting modern consumer goodies that even Greenlanders find attractive – after all, we do! Hunting's raison d'être has moved from a question of survival to being a business.

This is probably why so many fishermen and hunters keep their misgivings to themselves, concentrating instead on grabbing their share of the living resources before the party ends. Others blindly ignore all the data and vociferously deny that problems exist. Their views receive support from KNAPK, the trade union that consistently opposes any recommendation of restrictions in blazingly rhetorical terms.

And it is not just the 2,569 registered professional hunters who have raised the tempo. Many employed Greenlanders still regard themselves as 'hunters'. There are 8,094 leisure hunters who also want to hunt, shoot and fish in their spare time.

For many Greenlanders hunting remains an extremely important part of their life quality and identity. One example of this attitude was neatly expressed by Henrik Lund, the colourful mayor of the Qaqortoq/Julianehåb municipality, who retired from politics in April 2001. Apart from a spell of 4 years Henrik Lund had been king of the town since 1975. Asked what he would be doing now that he was retiring, he promptly replied: "*I hope to have more time to hunt Guillemots.*"

Finally, the 'industrialisation' of catches should not be forgotten. In the colonial era up to 1980 it was the Royal Greenland Trade Department (KGH) that set the rules governing the economic exploitation of living resources. Subsequently, the Greenland Home Rule Government has trudged along KGH's well-worn sledge trail, without so much as a sideways glance as to whether living resources are able to support this rising exploitation – or whether the exploitation is at all commercially viable.

The old KGH has simply been re-branded under names like Royal Greenland A/S, Nuka A/S and Great Greenland A/S. By and large these companies manage the purchasing, processing and export of all living resources in the country. These Home Rule Government owned companies receive annual subsidies running to millions of Danish kroner. Nevertheless, they operate at a loss.

In the financial year 1999/2000 the largest of these companies, Royal Greenland A/S, had a turnover in excess of DKK 3.5 billion. But profits were a meagre DKK 11 million. The previous year's profits had been no better – a measly DKK 10 million. Even these modest returns fail to take into account the cost of servicing the interest.

The Greenland Home Rule Government owns 100 per cent of Royal Greenland A/S and, amongst other things, it uses the company as an instrument for developing the labour market in Greenland. To this end, Royal Greenland A/S is subsidised by the Home Rule treasury – and here we are not talking of small change. For the financial year 1999/2000 the subsidy amounted to DKK 57 million.

But despite all this patronage, including a total subsidy of DKK 269 million for the period 1998–2002, Royal Greenland A/S is heavily debt-stricken to the tune of nearly DKK 3 billion. This is equal to the amount that Greenland receives from Denmark in annual block grants. There will be little room for any talk of sustainable exploitation if this debt is to be repaid from profits extracted from Greenland's living resources.

The fateful story of the Common Eider

Travelling several hundred years back in time would be the only way of experiencing the reality that lies behind the myth of an unspoilt Greenland.

Over exploitation began from the dawn of time. Even the earliest explorers wrote of rotting mounds of meat as a common feature at Inuit settlements. In modern times professional hunters are simply carrying forward the centuries-old tradition of taking any, and every, hunting opportunity – whether an animal is needed or not.

Thousands of seal carcasses are dumped back into the sea after skinning, and whale meat by the ton is simply abandoned on the ice once the tasty (and valuable) *mattak* has been flensed away. Having been shot Muskoxen are incinerated, and walrus carcasses are left lying after hunters have hacked off the heads with their large tusks. That is today's hunting reality.

In terms of meat-weight volumes Greenland's hunters kill birds and mammals in quantities that correspond to at least one and a half times the population's total meat consumption (see also p. 138, *Greenland meat account for 1998).*

The fate of the Eider is one of the best-documented examples of how wanton over exploitation wrecked stocks hundreds of years ago, when levels were far greater than they are today. This decimation was already complete some 160 years ago, and although Eiders reproduce at a faster rate than Brünnich's Guillemots, large colonies have never re-established themselves across most of Greenland. Migratory Canadian Eiders currently comprise a significant proportion of birds taken by hunters.

Unremittingly intensive hunting, unregulated collection of down and eggs together with other intrusions at nesting sites have effectively prevented numbers from picking up again. The Eider has a far better reproductive rate compared to the Brünnich's Guillemot, laying 3–6 eggs to the Guillemot's one. Denmark, amongst others, has shown that the introduction of hunting restrictions and the establishment of breeding sanctuaries is quickly rewarded by increased numbers of Eider.

Stocks were already overexploited in 1906 when Rasmus Müller published his 519-page opus *Vildtet og Jagten i Sydgrønland* (Wildlife and Hunting in Southern Greenland). Müller was the colony manager for Julianehåb, Godthåb, Holsteinsborg and several other areas, and he went to great lengths in his book to show that continuous all-year-round Eider hunting occurred everywhere. By using documents such as accounts ledgers showing the quantity of Eider down purchased during the 1800s, Müller proved that stocks had probably already collapsed before 1900!

But read for yourself what Müller wrote in 1906 about the Eider:

'No other bird is as profitable for Greenlanders as the Eider; the eggs and meat provide them with food, feathers and down provide them with money for other necessities of life, and the skins with down attached yield an excellent fur, which is partly used for clothes and partly turned into those highly-prized rugs. But nevertheless no other bird is so shamefully mistreated by them. On every windward headland that the birds have to pass on their morning and evening flights, a sharp shooter sits waiting, while out to sea Greenlanders lie in wait in kayaks and boats, blasting away at them. Exactly the same thing happens during the spring and autumn migrations. They seek out the places in kayaks where the birds dive for food then shoot or kill them with bird arrows. Even when the birds take refuge on the beaches hunters lying in ambush guarantee them a warm reception. In short, the birds get absolutely no peace anywhere, except in those remote places, which Greenlanders cannot reach during the winter. Luckily, there are many such places otherwise the Eider would certainly be extinct by now.

… Although, and especially in recent years, the number of Eider kills has undoubtedly been considerable, their numbers would scarely have diminished if the birds had been left in peace during the breeding season. Systematic destruction and disturbances during the breeding season are the main causes for the large decline in the number of birds, even though many have sought out alternative

and more peaceful breeding sites. Greenlanders are not just content to plunder the nests once – this practice might just be acceptable if birds were allowed to brood the second or third clutch undisturbed, because the Eider would then hatch at least 3 or 2 eggs – but instead they raid the nests two or three times, as often as the bird can lay a new clutch, leaving not a single egg behind. And even chicks recently hatched from their shells, fledglings found in the nests, which are worthless as food, even these are taken home for the hunter's children to play with. Mother ducks are shot near, and on their nests, rifled away from chicks irrespective of age. The birds literally cannot breed in peace except in those places inaccessible to Greenlanders. These are few and far between because hunters' kayaks and umiaks sail along the entire coastline and into all the fiords all summer long.'

Müller painstakingly researched the ledgers showing the annual purchases of Eider down in the nineteenth century. Two interesting facts emerge when comparing figures from specific years and various municipalities:

In the early 1800s far more Eiders were breeding in southern Greenland compared to the more northerly areas. Today the reverse situation applies. At the same time, throughout the century, numbers declined sharply both south and north. Between 1822–31 the average annual sale by weight of Eider down was 9,167 pounds. In the period 1887–1896, as the turn of the century approached, this annual average had declined to only 940 pounds.

Polar explorer Lauge Koch is another contemporary witness who described how, in the present northwest Greenland, Greenlanders destroyed countless Eider colonies at the beginning of the twentieth century. At that time people were migrating northwards from Upernavik and it was the Eider that suffered the consequences. Lauge Koch wrote about this exploitation in an article published in the journal *Meddelelser om Grønland* (1945), part of which is quoted below:

'Without the authorities noticing it, this population exterminated numerous eiderduck colonies on the outer islands between Tasiusak and Holms Ø. In the period 1916–23 the present author had the opportunity to observe this migration. Quite commonly a family chose an island with eiderduck colonies for

45

its summer camp site. This was of course very destructive to the eiderduck colonies of the islands. I have often visited Eskimo families in the winter who had cached several thousand eiderduck eggs, which were used as food for the dogs. In the early summer of 1923 I went in a motorboat to one of the outermost groups of islands within the district to examine whether eiderducks were breeding there. On my arrival I met an Eskimo family who had settled there, so even this remote eiderduck colony was going to be totally destroyed.'

The collection of Eider down and eggs from nests was permitted in the municipalities of Avanersuaq and Illoqqortoormiut/Scoresbysund until quite recently. New hunting regulations from January 2002 have finally put an end to the centuries old destruction of Eider colonies.

Brünnich's Guillemots and Saturday roast fever

In contrast to the historic destruction of Eider stocks, the drastic decline in the numbers of breeding Brünnich's Guillemots is more recent.

Stocks in Greenland were possibly stable up to 1950, but subsequently began to retreat. The decline really gathered momentum 25–30 years ago during the Salmon boom.

Year in, year out – while Salmon fever raged – hundreds of thousands of Brünnich's Guillemots drowned in the drifting nets that stretched kilometre after kilometre off the west coast of Greenland. In the period 1965–75 an estimated 200,000–500,000 Brünnich's Guillemots drowned in the Davis Strait – *every year*. Blood letting to the tune of 2–5 million birds in just 10 years must have had a considerable and negative impact on the Greenland breeding colonies, although this mass slaughter also affected a large number of Canadian birds. In the period 1983–87 Greenland's entire breeding stock numbered 539,000 birds.

Organized exploitation of bird colonies in Western Greenland is not merely a product of the past, or even colonial times.

For the Brünnich's Guillemot the starter's gun sounded in 1965.

That was the year when the Royal Greenland Trade Department (KGH) – allegedly *against* the wishes of local hunters – began purchasing and freezing Brünnich's Guillemots in the Upernavik municipality. Birds were exported to southern Greenland and also abroad. Older Danes fond of game can certainly remember the days when Danish shops sold frozen Brünnich's Guillemots alongside whale meat.

Brünnich's Guillemots were purchased in Upernavik over the following 10 years, but the total *numbers* of birds killed during these years is unknown. However, it was certainly larger than the numbers purchased because, as usual, hunters also shot birds for their own consumption. There is no doubt that the majority of frozen birds supplied for sale in KGH shops further to the south came from the most southern of Upernavik's Brünnich's Guillemot colonies. KGH purchases have probably played a considerable part in the total decline of these colonies, especially because birds arriving to breed were shot in May and June.

Brünnich's Guillemots (qty.) purchased by the KGH cold store in Upernavik 1965–75.

1965	17,337	1972	16,611
1966	1,416*	1973	17,468
1967	?	1974	10,232
1968	16,436	1975	2,553
1969	?	**total**	**92,127**
1970	10,074		
1971	?	average/year	11,516

*? No figures available. * Factory closed during part of summer.* Source: *Kampp, K. et al. 1994.*

Organized exploitation also took place on the east coast. In 1988 a small cold store opened in Illoqqortoormiut/Scoresbysund and began purchasing shot birds for export. The cold store was allocated a quota of 1,200 Brünnich's Guillemots in its first year. In 1990 the quota was increased to 1,250 birds. Since then, commercial purchasing is only permitted during the winter months in South and West Greenland.

Until recently KGH's successor, Royal Greenland A/S (owned by the Greenland Home Rule Government) has been responsible for the systematized purchase of Brünnich's Guillemots. Nowadays, NuKa A/S (another Home Rule owned company) has taken over most of this trade.

During the 1990s the Ministry of Fishing, Hunting and Agriculture authorised the commercial purchase of up to 25,000 Brünnich's Guillemots per season. Nearly half this quota was allocated to settlements in the Maniitsoq/Sukkertoppen and Paamiut/Frederikshåb municipalities. The remaining half of the quota went to settlements and outlying districts in South Greenland. According to Statistics Greenland the number of Brünnich's Guillemots purchased during recent years is as follows: 1997 – 19,722 birds; 1998 – 18,636 birds; 1999 – 18,194 birds.

Documentary evidence of this commercial hunt, based solely on birds taken during the *winter shooting season*, showed that for 1995/96 only one out of every 10 Brünnich's Guillemots purchased was an adult bird capable of breeding. The rest were juvenile birds. Although the numbers of birds killed were far greater than commercial purchases of Brünnich's Guillemots during *summer hunting* in Upernavik and Illoqqortoormiut/Scoresbysund, this type of exploitation is far less destructive to stocks. Summer hunting, in and near the guillemot colonies, particularly affects sexually mature Greenland birds because this is exactly the time when they are in the middle of producing the next generation. By contrast, winter hunting impacts mainly on non-fertile juveniles from abroad.

However, it has proved difficult to ensure sustainable exploitation in terms of stable sales of frozen Brünnich's Guillemots. For example, in autumn 1998, NuKa A/S had to drive two whole pallets with at least 2,000 Brünnich's Guillemots to the local dump in Paamiut/Frederikshåb. These birds from the 1997/98 hunting season were perfectly edible, but they were thrown out when new supplies of freshly killed Brünnich's Guillemot started arriving in town. Customers were no longer interested in buying frozen skinned birds as soon as they found they could buy fresh, ready-to-pluck birds.

Allowing for the fact that this may have been a locally isolated case, it nevertheless meant that about 10 per cent of the 1997/98 quotas were killed for no reason whatsoever. The paradox would be even more controversial if frozen Brünnich's Guillemots were also jettisoned in other municipalities. NuKa A/S pays hunters DKK 13 for every Brünnich's Guillemot, but even at that level the operation is unprofitable although the company declined to quantify the extent of its losses.

In addition, unknown quantities of fresh Brünnich's Guillemot are dumped in rubbish containers at the local 'brættet' markets held in larger towns. The carcasses end up being driven to the rubbish tip or incinerator. Supplies of fresh Brünnich's Guillemots to these markets are variable, and naturally they depend on the weather with the result that frequently there are more birds on offer than customers to buy them.

At the Nuuk/Godthåb market, fresh Brünnich's Guillemot typically costs DKK 30 per bird, but after a few days the price can plummet to DKK 10. When fresh supplies arrive, these unsold birds wind up in the container. Even special offers like 'Saturday roast fever – 10 for 100 kroner' cannot compete with customer demand for freshly-delivered birds. To a large extent this wastage stems from the total lack of connection between supply and demand. Professional hunters shoot everything they possibly can – and just hope for the best when it comes to sales.

This level of waste, which exists in every town, could easily run to thousands of birds. However, in terms of weight this is nothing compared to the thousands of tons of meat from seals, whales, Caribou, Muskoxen and fish that goes to rot. (See p. 138, *Greenland meat account for 1998.*)

Born environmentalists

There is a widespread notion in politically correct circles that Greenlanders and other Inuit groups live in perfect equilibrium with their natural environment.

The argument runs along the following lines: Animals are killed only when absolutely necessary. Otherwise, hunted animals are never disturbed. To maintain the balance between man and his environment Greenlanders have sacred places they protect – often in areas with abundant wild life. Traditional hunting rules are enforced specifying which animals can be hunted, who is allowed to hunt or eat particular animals, and thus society regulates the exploitation of natural resources.

In short by definition: The Inuit way of life is sustainable, and the Inuit are virtually born with a flair for sustainable exploitation of their surroundings. Hunting restrictions are therefore irrelevant because essential hunting is itself sustainable.

In the context of Greenland politics this argument is trotted out time after time. In 1992, Ussarqak Qujaukitsoq, a contemporary spokesman from Siumut (Greenland's largest political Party) made a statement in the Parliament that the Party '… *(has) repeatedly made it clear that our hunting culture is founded on an ecological awareness and the sustainable exploitation of resources. The country's most important profession has thus always been based on responsible management of these living resources …*'

Even then, the reality of the situation in Greenland contradicted this statement.

It was all a beautiful illusion, projected by well-meaning anthropologists and romantic nature lovers in western industrialised nations – aided, abetted and exploited by populist Greenland politicians and intellectuals. As recently as April 1997 the president of the Inuit Circumpolar Conference took to the speaker's rostrum at the United Nations in New York and made the following statement:

'(…) As a people we have neither lost our respect for the world of nature nor failed in our duty to treat it with respect. The Inuit have practised sustainable development for generations (…)'

The Inuit Circumpolar Conference (ICC) represents around 152,000 Inuit of Alaska, Canada, Russia and Greenland. The president is a Greenland career politician called Aqqaluk Lynge.

This myth is reiterated over and over again. As recently as Spring 2001, in a letter to the editor of Berlingske Tidende (one of Denmark's quality daily newspapers), one of Greenland's oldest politicians wrote:

'(…) Since days of old hunters have been famous for limiting their hunting when they sense that hunted animals and birds are in the danger zone (…).'

These words were penned by Otto Stenholdt, Member of Parliament and Greenland politician for 30 years. In Spring 2000 Otto Stenholdt was also the proposer and senior campaigner in Parliament's decision to introduce commercial egg collection – by any standards, a giant 30-year leap back in time.

Twelve years ago Finn Lynge formulated the doctrines adhered to by Ussarqak Qujaukitsoq, Aqqaluk Lynge and Otto Stenholdt. Finn Lynge is one of Greenland's most prominent intellectuals. Born in Nuuk in 1933, he was educated as a catholic priest in France, Rome and the USA. He is a former head of Radio Greenland, and as a Member of the European Parliament he prepared Greenland's withdrawal from the EU in 1985. Latterly, he was for some years the Inuit Circumpolar Conference's environment coordinator.

Although he lives in Helsingør, Denmark, Finn Lynge currently serves on The Commission on Self-Government for Greenland.

In his polemical book published in 1990 and entitled 'Kampen om de vilde dyr (The battle for wild animals)' Finn Lynge launched a full-blooded attack against environmentalist organisations that campaigned on behalf of hunted wild animals – especially seals. Of all the organisations singled out Greenpeace caught the full blast and to this day the 'Rainbow Warriors' are unpopular at almost every level of Greenland society.

The following excerpts are from '*Lifestyles*', the book's introductory chapter, in which Finn Lynge formulated the doctrine of sustainable Inuits living, as their forbears did, in harmony with nature:

'(…) Without any shadow of doubt, the most appropriate way for preserving areas of natural beauty is to safeguard the political and legal rights of those

people who have lived in these areas for hundreds of years in harmony with nature. Of all people they are the ones who have a clear and financial interest in ensuring that not one single animal species is wiped out.

(…) If only city-dwelling animal lovers could understand and realise that – in attempting to stem the tide of relentless and pointless destruction of wild nature and its animal life, taking place all over the world; in their desire to be able to pass on to their grandchildren a world full of beauty, life, and respect for all living creatures – they have no better allies than the fishing and hunting peoples who live the hunting life of their fathers on their ancestors' hunting grounds.'

The myth of the sustainable Inuit

It would of course be unreasonable to lay the entire responsibility for all this hereditary sustainability rhetoric – and the lack of follow-up action – at Finn Lynge's door. Nevertheless Lynge has played a major role in formulating and expounding the myth of the sustainable Inuit that has been trumpeted round society since 1990 – a myth that is abused politically and commercially in present day Greenland.

A very recent example of the rose-tinted picture can be found in the advertising material for sealskin products produced by Great Greenland A/S. This Greenland Home Rule owned company handles annual sales of about 100,000 sealskins. In its Spring 2001 press release the company reiterates the message of the sustainability of hunting in Greenland:

'A hunting tradition in harmony with nature
Life in Greenland is as different from our way of life as night is from day. It is difficult to imagine how people manage to live on a narrow band of rocky coast between the Ice Cap and the Arctic Ocean, where the summers are too short to cultivate cereals and vegetables, and where the temperature in winter can fall to -60° C. Hunting is vital for survival, providing both meat for food and fur for warm clothing.

The Greenlanders live and hunt as they have always done, for the seal has been hunted in Greenland just as long as there have been people there. Because of the total dependence on hunting for survival, Greenlanders have been careful never to take more animals than the balance of nature could bear. That is why the seal is NOT an endangered species in Greenland. Furthermore, the Greenlanders ONLY hunt the adult seal.

Originally, everything the Greenlanders had – apart from a little driftwood – was made from the animals they caught. To this very day, the meat is eaten and the skins are made into clothing. The dogs get the bones and other remains. The thought that nothing must go to waste is still deeply rooted in the Greenlanders.

In modern Greenland, sealskins are no longer used for some purposes, such as cladding kayaks and insulating huts, so there is a surplus of skins, which can be sold. With the money earned in this way, the Greenlanders can buy vegetables and other things that cannot be produced in Greenland.

Thereby Greenland sealskin is probably one of the few fur types, which can actually be called a bi-product. This fits well, with the attitude that many people have today – that we should live in harmony with nature. Just like the Greenland hunter has done for thousands of years.'

Source: *Great Greenland A/S web site, spring 2001,* www.great-greenland.gl

The anthropologist Frank Sejersen from the Department of Eskimology at the University of Copenhagen is one of the few professional academics who has tackled the thorny subject of the sustainable Inuit. In a lengthy article in the magazine 'Naturens Verden, 5/2000' he takes a critical look at the argument which claims that, even in modern times, the healthy exploitation of wildlife is part of a hunter's identity, underpinned by 'an intrinsic and hereditary environmental awareness in hunting cultures'.

Sejersen also discusses whether a traditional hunting culture has any contribution to make to the current debate on sustainability – a debate that primarily addresses the issue of limiting catches.

Using examples from the Arctic region Sejersen convincingly argues that prior to colonisation, traditional arctic hunters and trappers never thought about species' survival, but solely focused on their own. Currently, the considerations underpinning the management of living resources (and the term sustainable exploitation) are radically different from the way in which the Inuit traditionally regarded the hunting of animals.

Ostensibly there were three good reasons why the original population nevertheless lived 'sustainably', in equilibrium with the surrounding wildlife resources:

1. The Inuit peoples view of the world (naturalistic view)
2. The small population (only a few thousand people)
3. The very limited technology.

As Sejersen puts it: '*Perhaps, these parameters resulted in fewer animals caught with the numbers of animals killed posing no threat to stocks as they are called today. But there was no guaranteed outcome – in fact, this ideology could actually lead to over hunting. The hunting of animals was viewed from a completely different perspective at that time, and so it is questionable to talk in terms of environmental awareness based on our understanding of the term today.*'

These three parameters changed long ago, but nonetheless, with reference to hunting culture in the 'old days', politically correct spokespersons and populists confidently assert that Greenlanders' modern lives ought to be sustainable in relation to wildlife resources. The simplistically presented argument runs as follows: Essential hunting in its own right is sustainable – no matter whether stocks increase, decrease, or remain in balance.

Ideas on the theme of the 'sustainable Inuit' are not just peddeled by certain anthropologists, social scientists, politicians and Inuit intellectuals. One can hear the same claims being made in nearly all the rhetoric that deals with indigenous populations' understanding of wildlife and the exploitation of wildlife resources. Nowadays – and despite the fact that as time goes on examples of the opposite pile in from all over the world – there is still a widely held view in politically correct circles that indigenous peoples' culture is somehow perfectly adapted to wildlife and mother nature.

The view is based on the notion that indigenous peoples are part of the natural order, and that these primitive peoples live passively in the natural world, and are subjected to the same laws of nature, in the same way as animals. Viewed from this angle they are frozen in time so to speak, asserts Frank Sejersen. However, this perfect balance can be upset by the influence of Western culture on primitive peoples' way of life. Western industrial pollution can also disturb the balance of nature, but the sustainable Inuit alone cannot diminish or destroy natural resources – or words to that effect.

What lies behind these notions of primitive peoples' special understanding of nature? Reflecting just a little more deeply on these claims, they actually seem to be implying that indigenous peoples should be disconnected from, and not considered as, persons that actively reflect on, interact with, and change the course of nature, even though these same persons can relate to and change society. Indigenous peoples should be on a higher plane of some sort, but with animals' limited ability of reflection and independent will power.

Anyone who has visited modern day Greenland, even for a couple of hours, will know that the picture of Greenlanders as a harmonious non-interacting people in balance with their surroundings is absolute rubbish. Of course, one would be tempted to say.

In the real world, extreme cultures such as Greenland's are frequently much less in harmony with often-fragile surroundings than many well-developed industrial societies in far more robust ecosystems.

Frank Sejersen concludes his article with the following:

'(…) It is a problematic claim that traditional hunting cultures should be sustainable. In fact this type of crude assertion tears traditional hunting out of its cultural context. The traditional Inuit did not relate to animals as stock to be managed, but as active humanlike beings that returned year after year when their expectations were respected. It may well be that arguments about traditionalism, hunting culture and sustainability provide politico-ideological clout, but these arguments do no justice to local peoples' highly usable knowledge and vision. In fact this can lead to a kind of Jekyll and Hyde situation, where on the one hand present day problems need to be tackled, and on the other attempts are made to maintain the traditional sustainable hunting culture image. It is unproductive and unnecessary to look to the past for sources of inspiration for ensuring protection of hunted animals. Instead one ought to monitor, make the

most of, and extend present practices and types of cooperation, fully aware of the visions one has about landscape and resources, and review these in relation to modern society.(…)'

No respect for the law

Despite the fact that it makes obvious sense to protect living resources from over exploitation, the Greenland authorities have hitherto been unequal to the task.

To a great extent there is no tradition with regard to respecting restrictions. Ostensibly, this is deeply rooted in the culture, so much so that a Greenlander would not dream of upbraiding another Greenlander for inappropriate behaviour, far less protest against an offence.

In addition, we are talking about a very small society, where people prefer to coexist without police interference. Turning a blind eye on your neighbours' excesses makes for an easy life.

Only very infrequently do the Police receive notifications of violations of hunting laws and regulations, even though countless eyewitnesses have described breaches of these modest rules over many a past year. Brünnich's Guillemots are shot in July from boats ferrying doctors on call; Members of Parliament forage for breeding Eiders while sailing around coastal skerries; great whales are illegally shot at, or killed with rifles, and large quantities of eggs are collected from protected bird islands. Everyone notices but no one says anything. People do not get involved – and anyway it would not make much difference. This is a widespread attitude.

Angmalortoq Olsen from Sisimiut/Holsteinsborg is a rare exception. He was previously a works manager with the former cooperatively owned 'Sipeneq' company – the first production company in Greenland processing Greenlandic products for retail sale. When Parliament issued invitations in 1998 to a three-day seminar on the use of living resources, Angmalortoq Olsen sent a discussion paper to the seminar because – as he put it in his paper – "I would very much like my descendants to go hunting also." Here is an excerpt from Angmalortoq Olsen's lifelong experience of hunting and trapping:

'(…) The laws and rules that regulate exploitation of living resources are far too weak and toothless.

Offenders who break the law can be fined – but often only for repeated infringements.

Breaking the law in Denmark for example results in immediate confiscation of catches, equipment – even boats! Also, hunting permits, licenses, etc. are often revoked.

But this requires a willingness and ability to enforce laws and regulations. In Denmark the Police do the enforcement. Here, the Police are totally disinterested and the number of gamekeepers is scandalously few.

Laws and local by-laws are not worth the paper they are printed on if they cannot be enforced, or are not enforced at all.

On the contrary, respect for these laws and by-laws merely diminishes.

The way out of this mess is to have a more clearly defined version of laws and by-laws, and efficient enforcement.

Funds for employing more gamekeepers and fishery protection officers could perhaps come from raising the price of a hunting permit to between DKK 300–400. The price could also include public liability insurance while out hunting in a benefit similar to Danish hunting permits. Don't believe those who raise their hands in protest and claim that DKK 300 is far too high a price. A crate of beer costs more, and as far as I know no one protests about the price of beer! (…)'

The Chief Constable of Nuuk was unable to provide information as to whether fines for infringements of hunting and trapping laws had ever been made, and referred the enquiry to 'The Police Operations Report for Greenland in 2000'. Produced like a catalogue, this report on police work contains 150 pages, but there is not one single mention of this type of offence. However, there were many detailed statistics on: paternity cases, suicides, murders, deaths by drowning, accidental shootings, rescue operations, numbers of driving licenses issued, burglaries, drug-related crimes, etc. Neither has the Danish Ministry of Justice any knowledge of these types of hunting and trapping offences in Greenland.

Even the Greenland Police are themselves not always a model of restraint. In the summer of 1995 an inhabitant of Paamiut/Frederikshåb reported a policeman for illegally collecting Arctic Tern eggs. The police officer, who was on-duty carrying out trout inspection controls, returned to Paamiut harbour on the evening of 27 July, bringing with him 30 fresh Arctic Tern eggs.

Hunting regulations specifically prohibit the collection of Arctic Terns' eggs after 1 July.

The Chief Constable of Nuuk sanctioned an investigation but 6 months later the person who reported the offence received a note to the effect that: 'The case was shelved because of lack of evidence.'

In citing the reason for his decision, The Chief Constable stated that the officer in question had denied the charges and explained that the Tern eggs were hard-boiled and had been in his dinghy for at least 27 days since the end of June.

Children – hunting they will go

Hunting pressure is enormous in Greenland. One in every five Greenlanders possesses either a professional hunting permit (2,569 persons), or a leisure-hunting permit (8,094 persons). According to Statistics Greenland the annual import of ammunition for shotguns and rifles amounts to 90 tons, equivalent to 9 kilos of ammunition per hunter.

Greenlanders have to comply with very few formal requirements to be able to go hunting or trapping. Hunters only need to be over 12 years old, and be registered in the local municipality. Hunters can apply for a permit to shoot Caribou and Muskox once they turn 16.

Hunting tests are non-existent. No form of documented knowledge is required from children, or leisure and professional hunters about the animals hunted, rules and regulations (including hunting seasons), or knowledge on safety and how to handle hunting weapons responsibly.

These days, in most other countries, hunting proficiency and rifle tests are obligatory.

In Denmark, would-be hunters have to pass a theoretical and practical test to obtain an ordinary hunting permit. They are also obliged to pass a special rifle test if they want to use a sporting rifle. The test involves hitting a 20 cm target at a distance of 100 metres with 5 out of 6 shots. Applicants consistently need to demonstrate their abilities to treat firearms safely and responsibly.

In Sweden, there are two types of rifle tests, apart from the test to acquire a hunting permit. In the most difficult of these, (the advanced big game test for hunting Elk and Deer) correct answers have to be given to 25 out of 30 theoretical questions. The test thereafter involves shooting at moving and standing targets, with the pass requirement being 3 hits for every 4 shots.

Hunters in Norway have to pass an *annual* rifle test prior to the Elk and Reindeer hunting season. Here 5 out of 5 shots must hit the target (30 centimetres in diameter) at a distance of 100 metres. Canada also has regulations for implementation of safety courses prior to firearms being used for hunting and trapping.

Hunting by motorboat was the usual practice. This type of hunting involved surprising or overtaking birds on the water in high-speed dinghies with 70–90 HP engines, but under the revised Bird Game Law enforceable from 1 January 2002 the shooting of birds from moving motorboats has been banned.

Greenlanders are the only people in the world permitted by the International Whaling Commission (IWC) to kill *large whales* with rifles. This often involves a very protracted kill, which is clearly unacceptable from an animal welfare viewpoint.

Seals can be shot all year round with the exception of the Harbour Seal, which is protected in the summer. Belugas, Narwhals and smaller whales like Harbour Porpoises and Pilot Whales have no close season whatsoever. The rare *Walrus* is protected south of latitude 66°N, where it is hardly ever found. Walrus hunting is permitted from March–April between latitudes 66°N and 70°30'N. North of 70°30'N, and in the whole of East Greenland south of the National Park, Walruses are protected all year round. Hunting times, and rules covering hunting methods, are often laid down locally for individual species: See species lists in chapter 3.

Greenland's hunting laws permit the *collection of eggs*. Until recently everyone has been allowed to collect the eggs of the following species for personal consumption before 1 July: Northern Fulmar, Arctic Tern, Arctic Skua, Great black-backed Gull, Iceland Gull, Glaucous Gull, Black-legged Kittiwake, Black Guillemot and Little Auk.

But since January 2002 a new Bird Game Law has shortened the list of species to: Northern Fulmar, Great black-backed Gull and Glaucous Gull, and shortened the open season to stop before 1 June. However, in the Avanersuaq and Illoqqortoormiut/Scoresbysund municipalities people can still collect Little Auk eggs throughout the whole breeding season.

Commercial egg collection is permitted. Professional hunters can collect the eggs of Great black-backed Gull and Glaucous Gull and sell them locally before 1 June.

The main problem associated with egg collection in Greenland is the repeated disturbance of birds throughout the entire breeding season. If the local population could agree to organize egg collection on the basis of one annual visit, the extent of the damage would probably be limited. This is the system used in the Faroe Islands, where exploitation of specified bird cliffs is a kind of private right of ownership.

Egg collection is the overwhelmingly dominant reason for Greenland losing the world's largest colony of 50,000–80,000 breeding pairs of Arctic Terns. Finn Salomonsen, the well-known Danish zoologist described the damaging effects of this type of unfettered egg collection as far back as 1967:

'Previously about 100,000 eggs were collected annually from one of the largest breeding grounds at Grønne Ejland in Disko Bay. This is now no longer possible because Arctic Tern numbers both here and in many other places have declined due to constant disturbance of their breeding grounds.'

In 1996 the Greenland Institute of Natural Resources carried out a thorough census of bird numbers on Grønne Ejland in Disko Bay. Survey results revealed that a mere 5,000 breeding pairs of Arctic Terns remained.

The report by the Greenland Institute of Natural Resources also pointed out that 150–200 persons from the local community visited the islands to collect tern eggs during the census in June 1996. Collection buckets presumably also contained eggs from several pairs of Long-tailed Skuas and the extremely rare Ross's Gull, which had one of its few Greenland breeding grounds on Grønne Ejland. In the summer of 2000 the Ministry of Environment and Nature repeated some of the 1996 census: Not a single Arctic Tern nest with eggs or chicks was found.

Greenland's most southerly colony of Brünnich's Guillemots is also plagued by egg collection. According to biologists from the Greenland Institute of Natural Resources the population of Brünnich's Guillemots at Ydre Kitsissut in the Qaqortoq/Julianehåb municipality has declined by around 37 per cent in the space of just 7 years. Ydre Kitsissut is one of the few protected birdlife sites where shore landings during the breeding season have been prohibited since 1978. Nevertheless, in 1999, biologists found unmistakable traces of repeated violations.

Selling collected eggs is expressly forbidden by law, but in Spring 2000 Parliament voted unanimously to legalize commercial egg collection. Professional hunters were granted permits to collect and sell the eggs of two species of gulls. The decision to allow commercial egg collection was taken despite warnings from the Greenland Institute of Natural Resources which feared the consequences of increased pressure on many species of birds. The problem is not these two species of gulls, but the risk that eggs from many other species will be collected, and that egg collecting will lead to repeated disturbances of bird colonies.

Downhill all the way

The grim reality

'We should not hunt so much that stocks decline. In other words we must not simply harvest the income but must also retain the capital as an investment we can pass on to our descendants.'

Statement by Premier Jonathan Motzfeldt to the Greenland Home Rule Parliament 'Seminar on living resources', in Nuuk/Godthåb 9 October 1998.

The collective picture of wildlife 'living resources' in Greenland – mammals, birds, fish and crustaceans – currently reveals that the populations of almost all species are highly diminished. Heavy exploitation and outright over-exploitation has nearly or completely wiped out certain stocks. Profits continue to be made on capital investments as if the end of the world was near.

However, there are solitary bright spots in an otherwise gloomy picture. Management of stocks of *Deep Sea Shrimp*, *Caribou* and *Muskox* (in West Greenland) has demonstrated that it is apparently possible to regulate and control hunting pressure, so that capital investments are not frittered away.

This chapter examines the commercial and culturally interesting species of hunted animals. The narrative, which is primarily based on technical reports from the Greenland Institute of Natural Resources, sets out soberly and competently to show what is known, and what is not known about Greenland's living resources. In addition, data has been obtained from the Ministry of Industry, Grønlands Skindindhandling (Greenland Fur Traders), Statistics Greenland, Radio Kalaallit Nunaata/Radio Greenland, the printed press in Greenland, and international media, together with many other scientific sources.

An arrow in black after the species name in Latin indicates whether the population is on the increase ↑, stable →, or declining ↓. A question mark? indicates that there is insufficient information about a species' situation to make a statement with certainty. The author's use of symbols is based on currently available information.

For an overall list of animal population trends see chapter 1, p. 15.

Bird species

Exploitation of bird stocks is regulated by the Greenland Home Rule Government through Ministry of Environment and Nature rules that stipulate hunting seasons, methods and types of hunting equipment, etc.

International conventions, scientific commissions and cooperation agreements increasingly play a part in the management of pan-continental bird populations. With a view to sustainable exploitation in the future, Greenland has undertaken to collect information about its bird stocks as part of its arctic environmental cooperation with CAFF (*Conservation of Arctic Flora and Fauna*).

Brünnich's Guillemot *(Uria lomvia)* ↓

Brünnich's Guillemots breed in 21 colonies along the west coast of Greenland from Ydre Kitsissut in the south to Hakluyt Island in the north. More than half the breeding population is located in 5 colonies in the sparsely populated Avanersuaq municipality of North Greenland. In East Greenland there are only two colonies, both at Illoqqortoormiut/Scoresbysund.

Today, all colonies in the Uummannaq municipality are extinct – including the famous one at the Salleq bird cliff. Brünnich's Guillemot populations have declined from approx. 500,000 birds to fewer than 10,000 during the last 60 years in the area between Disko Bay and Upernavik Isfjord. In 1994 a census of Greenland's breeding population recorded 535,000 individuals, corresponding to approx. 375,000 breeding pairs.

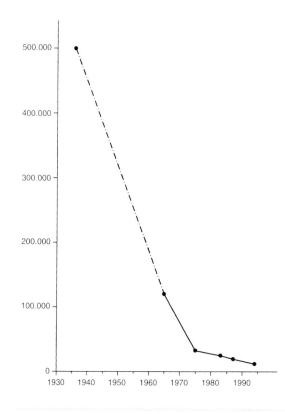

The reduction in the population of Brünnich's Guillemots between Disko Bay and Upernavik Isfjord in northwest Greenland symbolises all too acutely the general impoverishment of Greenland's wildlife over the last 60 years. Populations have declined from about half a million birds to less than 12,000 as a result of hunting during the breeding season. Source: Topografisk Atlas Grønland, Copenhagen 2000.

There is no doubt that over exploitation, especially in the form of illegal large-scale *summer hunting,* is the reason for this dramatic decline over the last fifty years. Egg collection also plays a part, as described in Chapter 2, p. 59 ff.

According to official hunting statistics recorded by *Piniarneq* since 1993, between 188,000 and 255,000 Brünnich's Guillemots are shot every year in Greenland, but the figure is misleading.

Two studies on sales of Brünnich's Guillemots in Nuuk in the 1990s clearly indicated that more than twice as many Brünnich's Guillemots were killed than were reported to the statisticians. There was also evidence that in some settlements more Brünnich's Guillemots were purchased alone for commercial resale than the total numbers reported to *Piniarneq*.

When this shortfall in reporting is taken into account, the official total would need to be corrected to 400,000–500,000 Brünnich's Guillemots killed annually.

It goes without saying that a breeding population of approx. 375,000 pairs cannot survive hunting pressure of 400,000–500,000 birds annually – particularly in the case of birds reproducing as slowly as Brünnich's Guillemots. It is also well known that Greenlandic hunters and leisure hunters kill very large numbers of birds from Brünnich's Guillemot colonies in other countries.

Brünnich's Guillemots are the most important birds hunted in Greenland, despite having a life style that makes them unsuited to hunting. The birds only start breeding after five years development, and each pair produces only one chick at the most (an average of only 0.7 chicks per breeding pair).

By comparison, over a five-year period, a breeding pair of Rock Ptarmigan is capable of contributing 3,000 individuals – so long as all the offspring survive. On average, over a similar period, a pair of Brünnich's Guillemots can produce just five and a half offspring. Clearly Brünnich's Guillemot populations can only tolerate very limited and sustainably-based exploitation if breeding populations are not to decline. In fact, to prevent such a decline, year on year adult survival rates need to be around 90 per cent. Shooting, or creating other unnecessary noise nearer than 5 kilometres to breeding colonies has been prohibited for many years for exactly these reasons.

North of Kangaatsiaq municipality Brünnich's Guillemots are protected from 16 February–31 August, but in the Avanersuaq municipality, where the majority of Greenland birds are breeding, the close season only lasts from 16 June–31 August (however, before 1 January 2002 hunting was allowed in Avanersuaq and Illoqqortoormiut/Scoresbysund municipalities all year round). South of Kangaatssiaq a close season operates from 16 February–14 October.

Countless examples show that these limited close seasons are not respected (chapter 2, p. 32 ff., and other references). Local hunters in small dinghies sail right under the steep bird cliffs, where they shoot breeding birds in large numbers with rifles or shotguns.

Hunting quotas are non-existent, though leisure hunters are only allowed to shoot a maximum of 5 birds per hunting trip for their own consumption. Additionally, there are rules governing types of firearms and means of transport that can be used. Nevertheless, hunting regulations are violated on a massive scale because law enforcement is so feeble.

Winter hunting of Brünnich's Guillemots has reached such proportions that it contributes to bird cliffs being emptied in Greenland – and possibly other countries as well. Greenland's Brünnich's Guillemots overwinter mainly around Newfoundland, while Russian, Norwegian, Icelandic and Canadian Brünnich's Guillemots spend the winter off West Greenland. Brünnich's Guillemots from Spitsbergen predominate south of Paamiut in a wintering area where Greenland birds are seldom found. So birds from other countries particularly bear the brunt of winter hunting.

In the autumn of 2000 Iceland placed the Brünnich's Guillemot on its Endangered Species list. From 1985–1994 significant declines in the numbers of breeding pairs were recorded, amounting to 2.7 per cent and 4.1 per cent respectively – *annually* – for the two Icelandic colonies that were monitored during the census. Inclusion on the Endangered Species list is the direct result of 'excessive winter hunting in West Greenland and Newfoundland'. By all accounts, hunting pressure on Brünnich's Guillemots from Svalbard is at least as intensive as hunting pressure on Iceland's overwintering visitors.

Over exploitation of Brünnich's Guillemots in winter quarters has long been recognised as a serious problem. Drastic reductions in hunting quotas and commercial trading were implemented years ago in Newfoundland. As part of the CAFF program, Greenland has undertaken to contribute to the monitoring and management of the Brünnich's Guillemot population on the grounds that the birds' migration habits are of joint concern to Arctic nations.

Common Eider *(Somateria mollissima)* ↓

Mainly extinct around all major towns and settlements these birds breed in small numbers scattered throughout Greenland. No overall information is available about breeding populations, which in 1996 were estimated to consist of 10,000–100,000 breeding pairs. Populations have declined drastically in the few breeding locations where censuses have been conducted in recent times.

Intensive hunting is the predominant reason for the current decline, but egg and down collection also plays a role. An additional factor is disturbance. Today, the characteristic feature is that the few intact colonies are situated far away from populated areas.

Over 160 years ago, around 1840, the quantity of Eider down sold by Greenland hunters indicated that there were at least 110,000 breeding pairs in West Greenland. According to sales ledgers, twice as much down was purchased from South Greenland as from North Greenland, which at that time did not include the Avanersuaq municipality. Historically it is probably the case that Eider populations were more concentrated in the south than in the north. The reverse situation applies today. This historical over exploitation is described in chapter 2, p. 43 ff.

The winter population of Eiders in open sea areas off west Greenland is also largely unknown. As the Eider is mainly a non-migratory bird in Greenland, it is assumed that the entire West Greenland breeding population overwinters in open sea areas. Additionally, the winter population is supplemented by an unknown, though sizeable, number of birds from Canadian breeding grounds. It is presumed that at least part of the Devon and Ellesmere Islands' population migrates to Greenland. Discoveries of ringed birds confirm sizeable migrations of birds from Hudson Bay and Hudson Strait. During the period 1996–2001 34 ringed Eiders from this area were found in Greenland. There are considerable grounds for believing that large numbers of Eider shot in Greenland originate from Canada.

Greenland's north-eastern population is not affected by winter hunting as it overwinters around Iceland, where birds cannot be hunted.

Actually, not much is known about the size and development of arctic Eider populations. However, in scientific circles, there are considerable concerns for the future of Eider populations, which are subjected to enormous hunting pressures everywhere, from the breeding grounds in Nunavut to overwintering sites in Quebec, Labrador, Newfoundland and Greenland. The incidence of arctic Eiders with lead shot in their bodies is extremely high, supporting the view that these populations are hunted very intensively. A survey made of breeding females in colonies in Newfoundland and Labrador revealed that 39 per cent and 54 per cent respectively of birds flying had lead shot in their bodies!

Hunting pressure in Greenland has been very severe for more than fifty years. During the period 1948–51 the Greenland Administration of the day compiled statistics showing that on average 144,000 Common Eiders were shot annually. However, these figures do include an unknown percentage of King Eiders.

Nowadays, about 80 per cent of total Eider kills are shot in the open sea areas off West Greenland. According to official hunting statistics recorded by *Piniarneq* since 1993, 66,000–83,500 Common Eiders are shot annually. However, these figures are far from accurate. Firstly, it is highly likely that a considerable number of kills are under-reported (see also the section on Brünnich's Guillemots). Secondly, the large number of maimed birds is unknown. Many die later and are not included in the statistics.

Confusing Common Eider with King Eider (referred to in the next section) redresses the balance somewhat in the opposite direction because thousands of King Eider kills are mistakenly reported as if they were Common Eider.

Eiders are protected throughout Greenland during the period 16 February–14 October (before 1 January 2002 the close season was only 1 July–15 August/30 September). Anyone with a valid professional hunting permit can shoot unlimited numbers of Eiders during the shooting season. Professional hunters are also permitted to sell/purchase unlimited numbers of birds. Leisure hunters are only allowed to shoot a maximum of 5 birds per hunting trip for their own consumption (from 1 January 2002).

In other arctic areas there is considerable unease about the negative population trends. As a result, countries (including Greenland) that cooperate under the *'Arctic Environmental Protection Strategy (AEPS)'* have increasingly focused on Eider stock management. It has been decided that, after Brünnich's Guillemots, Eider species will have top priority in connection with any joint action. Not surprisingly, what lies behind this decision is Canada's emphatic protest concerning the decline of its breeding populations.

Conservation of Arctic Flora and Fauna (CAFF) has produced a protection plan for all species of Eider in the arctic region. With an eye on more sensible stock management in the future, many arctic countries (including Greenland) have started extensive studies of their indigenous Eider populations.

King Eider *(Somateria spectabilis)* ↓

King Eiders breed in relatively unknown numbers only in North and Northeast Greenland in contrast to Common Eiders, which breed throughout Greenland.

Greenland is a vitally important moulting area (summer), and an overwintering site for Canadian breeding birds. It is estimated that at least 270,000 King Eiders roost around Greenland during the winter.

Hunting kills in Greenland are unknown. True, the Home Rule Government's official statistics issued by *Piniarneq* record the shooting of a mere 4,000–5,500 King Eiders annually, equivalent to 6–7 per cent of official Common Eider kills, but these figures are far below the real numbers.

Firstly, similar to Brünnich's Guillemots, it is highly probable that the numbers of Common and King Eiders killed are far larger than the actual reported numbers. In this scenario actual kills could be more than twice as great.

Significant under-reporting of King Eider kills on account of mistaken identities compounds this issue. Surveys of Eider species from kills on sale in Nuuk/Godthåb during the winter of 1995/96 indicated that the actual proportion of King Eiders is much higher. The survey revealed that King Eiders accounted for 32 per cent of all Eiders sold.

Applying this percentage to total Eider kills indicates that a minimum of 24,000–28,500 King Eiders are killed annually – equivalent to nearly 10 per cent of the estimated winter population of at least 270,000 birds. Assuming that under-reporting of kills of Common and King Eider occurs at the same level as Brünnich's Guillemots, then the annual catch rises to at least 48,000–57,000 King Eiders – nearly 20 per cent of the winter population.

These kill numbers constitute a very high proportion of the total world population. For years it has been common knowledge that Greenland kills placed serious strains on breeding populations in eastern Canada. Canadians have repeatedly and sharply criticised hunting in Greenland, but so far to no avail.

In Greenland the close season for King Eiders now operates from 16 February–14 October (before 1 January 2002 only during the summer from 1 July–15 August).

A large segment of the world's total population of King Eiders moults and overwinters at foraging sites in West Greenland. Consequently, it is a major problem when these locations are unusable by birds due to the presence of Scallop fishermen or unregulated hunters.

A good example is the previously very important moulting site at Aqajarua/Mudderbugten in Disko Bay, which was number one on the 1987 Greenland list of Ramsar designated sites. In former times this location was the August habitat for 30,000 moulting King Eiders, but today the area is insignificant as a moulting site. This is due to hunting, disturbances and Scallop fishing. The location's official status as a designated Ramsar site has been irrelevant, as the Ramsar Convention has never been implemented under Greenland law.

Arctic Tern *(Sterna paradisaea)* ↓

Breeds throughout Greenland, though most colonies are found in West Greenland. However the species is missing along hundreds of kilometres of coastline. For example there are only three small colonies along the entire coast between Nunap Isua/Kap Farvel and Paamiut/Frederikshåb.

There are good reasons to assume that total populations have declined drastically during the last hundred years. The reasons: Excessive egg collection and disturbances during the breeding season.

Today, egg collecting is viewed as the dominant reason why Greenland has lost, amongst other things, the world's largest colony of Arctic Terns on the Grønne Ejland group of islands. Around 1950 estimates suggested the presence of 50,000–80,000 breeding pairs, but in the summer of 2000 not a single successful breeding pair was recorded.

According to the research figures a total of about 30,000 breeding *individuals* have been recorded in West Greenland. Current estimates for the entire population suggest a maximum 30,000–60,000 breeding birds for the whole of Greenland. This is fewer than the number of birds previously breeding on Grønne Ejland in Disko Bay.

Ironically, even in 1987 Grønne Ejland was put on the protected list of Ramsar sites in Greenland – with special reference to the large Arctic Tern population that was to be protected under the Ramsar Convention's rules covering disturbances of locations during breeding seasons. Not surprisingly this designation never had any practical significance, as the Ramsar Convention has never been implemented under Greenland law.

Before 1 January 2002 egg collection for private consumption was permitted until 1 July – despite the fact that Arctic Terns were totally protected throughout Greenland. However, this protection was never respected and many colonies were visited after 1 July. This resulted in eggs being collected throughout the entire breeding season. Today egg collection is prohibited. Read more about this in Chapter 2, p. 59 ff.

It can be expected that the situation will not improve following Parliament's unanimous vote in the spring of 2000, to allow the commercial collection and sale of eggs. This decision was taken despite warnings from the Greenland Institute of Natural Resources, which forecast an increased pressure on bird colonies. True, only professional hunters have the right to collect eggs, and permits apply to only two species of gull. However, it is feared that greater disturbance will occur, and also that both intentional and unwitting collection and selling of eggs will also affect Arctic Terns and other protected species of birds.

Geese ↑

Six different species of Geese are commonly found in Greenland. These are: **Pink-footed Goose** (*Anser brachyrhynchus*), **White-fronted Goose** (*Anser albifrons flavirostris*), **Snow Goose** (*Anser caerulescens atlanticus*), **Canada Goose** (*Branta canadensis cf. interior*), **Barnacle Goose** (*Branta leucopsis*) and **Brent Goose** (*Branta bernicla hrota*).

All the populations migrate long distances from their breeding grounds in Greenland to wintering sites in either north-west Europe or the USA.

The majorities of European and North American goose populations are increasing, or stable following an increase. This is linked to the fact that geese have started to winter feed in cultivated areas, and that hunting pressure at wintering sites has been considerably regulated.

The Greenland Pink-footed Goose, Snow Goose and Canada Goose belong to large populations (>100,000 birds), and are divided bi-nationally (either Iceland-Greenland or Canada-Greenland). All populations are increasing in Greenland both in terms of numbers and distribution.

By contrast, White-fronted Goose and Barnacle Goose populations are small (25,000–100,000 birds), and their breeding areas are distributed over a small number of sites in Greenland. For this reason Greenland has a special responsibility for these breeding populations.

Finally there is the Brent Goose. Found in two distinct populations in Greenland, stocks are very small (5,000–25,000 birds) and vulnerable. All birds from the Canadian population migrate via Greenland both in spring and autumn and a considerable proportion – up to 25 per cent – of the Svalbard population lives in the most eastern part of North Greenland during the summer. The total Svalbard population in winter 1996/97, including birds from Greenland, numbered about 6,000 birds. Protection of these stocks and their habitats is therefore of paramount importance for the birds' survival.

Hunting the Pink-footed Goose, Barnacle Goose and White-fronted Goose is permitted in Greenland, but all other species of geese are unconditionally protected. Before 1 January 2002 the hunting season was long, and shooting of these three species of geese was legal during spring migrations – right up to their breeding grounds.

Today a close season for shooting *Pink-footed Goose* operates from 1 June–31 August. In the Illoqqortoormiut/Scoresbysund municipality on the east coast, a close season only operates from 1 July–31 August. A close season for *Barnacle Goose* operates from 1 May-31 August, but in the Illoqqortoormiut/Scoresbysund municipality from 1 July–31 August. For *White-fronted Goose* a close season now operates from 16 October–31 August in all Greenland. It is worth remembering though that all species of geese migrate away from Greenland during the winter.

The hunting pressure on the Pink-footed and Barnacle Goose is assumed to be limited as in practice these are only shot in the east coast Illoqqortoormiut/Scoresbysund district. During the 1980s it was estimated that the total number of geese shot in that area was between 500–1,000. In reality there are no accurate estimates about the numbers of geese killed at the present time.

In practice the White-fronted Goose has only been hunted in West Greenland and mainly during autumn months, but there is little information about kill sizes. According to hunting statistics recorded since 1993, a mere 1,100–2,000 'geese' are recorded as being shot, but unfortunately no distinction is made between different species of geese.

The North and Northeast Greenland National Park is of major importance for the breeding populations of Pink-footed Goose, Barnacle Goose and Brent Goose. For this reason it is important that consideration is shown for sites used by geese during raw material exploration in the National Park, especially if activity increases.

A large number of primary geese locations appear on the list of designated Ramsar sites in both East and West Greenland. However, as long as Ramsar convention articles are not implemented, protection of these areas remains purely theoretical.

Finally the Bureau of Minerals and Petroleum has identified a range of 'important wild life sites', but regulations for these areas only cover mineral exploration. Commercial production of raw materials requires separate environmental approvals, which need to take wild-life habitats into account.

Marine mammals

Whereas management of bird stocks is handled by the Ministry of Environment and Nature, catch regulations and quotas for marine mammals are administered by the Ministry of Industry.

In 1992, Norway, Iceland, the Faroe Islands and Greenland formed NAMMCO, the North Atlantic Marine Mammal Commission. Amongst other things, this scientific collaboration advises on the management of small whales, Walruses and seals. However, the International Whaling Commission (IWC) – including Denmark as the formal member state – specifies annual catch quotas for large whales in Greenland.

Belugas and Narwhals are not covered by IWC quota allocations, but are managed directly by the Ministry of Industry. Scientific data concerning these species is collected by JCCM, (Canada-Greenland Joint Commission for the Conservation and Management of Narwhal and Beluga). Polar Bear populations are managed by regulations set out in the 1973 Oslo Convention.

Polar Bear *(Ursus maritimus)* ↓?

In Greenland Polar Bears move with the sea ice. Consequently, Polar Bears frequently appear along the entire east coast of Greenland and in Northwest Greenland. Sightings of Polar Bears in Southwest Greenland fluctuate greatly because the bears move with the pack ice from East Greenland. Polar Bears are only rarely found along open sea coastal areas between Paamiut/Frederikshåb and Nuuk/Godthåb and along Greenland's northern coast adjoining the Arctic Ocean.

According to the *Piniarneq 2001* official hunting statistics, 121–198 Polar Bears are killed annually in the whole of Greenland, though these figures do not adequately reflect the actual numbers killed. The estimated figure is higher. Polar Bear hunters are required to submit detailed information about every single kill under Greenland Home Rule regulations for Polar Bear hunting, but in the majority of cases this information is never submitted. In actual fact no one knows how many animals are killed each year.

Information regarding the prevalence of Polar Bears in *East Greenland* is so inadequate that international biologists are reluctant to publish figures on population sizes. The number of kills, information about the bears' origins, and size of the exploited population are unknown, and estimates are impossible as to whether kills are made on a sustainable basis.

For *West Greenland* official figures reveal that, on average, five Polar Bears are shot every year in this south-western region. These are bears, which come ashore from the East Greenland pack ice. In the remainder of West Greenland, the bear population is 'shared' with Canada where the species is also hunted. It is generally accepted that the population is made up of three largely distinct groups. The number of kills made in common territories is estimated to be approximately 117 animals annually, with Greenland hunters accounting for about fifty animals. This figure is regarded as being more or less sustainable, although the trend is 'somewhat higher than the calculated sustainable exploitation level'.

Unlike Canada, hunting in Greenland is not subject to quota restrictions. However, killing Polar Bears is only allowed for sheep farmers and hunters with valid professional hunting permits. The use of poison, gin traps or foot snares, and auto-firing guns (lethal trip-wire-activated weapons) is prohibited. Polar Bear hunting by plane, helicopter, snow-scooter and motorised transport is also banned.

Lone male bears can be hunted all year round, while the remainder of bears are protected by a close season operating in July and August. However, In Tasiilaq/Ammassalik municipality the close season is in August and September. These restrictions do not apply to locations with flocks of sheep. Bears can be shot here all year round. Important Polar Bear areas are located in Melville Bay and the North and Northeast Greenland National Park.

Polar Bears are included under Article II of the CITES Convention for regulating international trade of animals and animal products. This requires mandatory approval of every single export of Polar Bear products. Moreover, Greenland is committed to manage its Polar Bear stocks in cooperation with other Polar Bear countries through the *International Agreement for Preservation of Polar Bears and their Habitats* (Oslo Convention of 1973). In autumn 2000, The Greenland Home Rule Government committed itself in principle to tighten Polar Bear hunting regulations with quotas and quota allocations along the same lines as Beluga and Narwhal catches (see p. 89). However, negotiations on quota allocations have been provisionally postponed until spring 2002.

Canada has an efficient management regime for regulating Polar Bear stocks and hunting. Amongst other aspects, this system is based on yearly adjustments to local quotas to ensure that a proper balance of adult females is maintained. To determine an animal's age hunters are required to submit a jawbone for every Polar Bear shot, and in the case of male animals, submit the baculum to confirm the bear's sex. If the latter is not submitted, the killed animal is counted as a female and next year's quotas are subsequently reduced by one animal.

Seals

Five species of seals of interest to hunters are found along Greenland's coastline.

These are: **Ringed Seal** (*Phoca hispida*), **Harbour Seal** (*Phoca vitulina concolor*), **Bearded Seal** (*Erignathus barbatus*), **Harp Seal** (*Phoca groenlandica*) and **Hooded Seal** (*Cystophora cristata*).

The Harbour Seal is the only species of seal in obvious decline. The others are presumed to be either stable or increasing, despite extensive killing of several species.

Kill statistics published in Piniarneq 2001. (1993–1998, smallest and largest numbers per year):

Ringed Seal	76,935–89,782
Harbour Seal	217–295
Bearded Seal	1,800–2,354
Harp Seal	56,660–82,491
Hooded Heal	6,957–9,888

According to *Piniarneq 2001* the reported annual seal kill for Greenland is 150,000–173,000 animals. Based on records from Grønlands Skindindhandling (Greenland Fur Traders), sealskin purchases accounted for about two thirds of this figure. The sealskin trade has doubled over the past twenty years and today the scale of kills in Greenland has probably never been higher.

Since 1980 the Greenland Home Rule Government has bankrolled professional and leisure hunters by increasing the subsidies for sealskin purchases. These subsidies, fixed every year by the Greenland Finance Act peaked in 1999 with grants totalling DKK 44.4 million for the purchase of 106,100 skins (approx. 50 per cent Harp Seals, 47 per cent Ringed Seals, and 3 per cent other species).

Amongst other things this system guarantees the purchase of all sealskins brought in by hunters. This is why the volume of sealskin purchases is far higher than the numbers that can be resold on world markets. The result: Growing stockpiles at the Government owned Grønlands Skindindhandling.

Meanwhile the quality of purchased sealskins has fallen dramatically over the last decade. In 1999 alone, 20 per cent of the skins had to be rejected. The generous subsidy (DKK 364 average for every seal in 2000) is the primary reason why kills are on the increase. It also means that thousands of seals are shot merely for the sake of their skins, with their carcasses dumped into the sea after skinning. Apparantly, how to use or sell this considerable quantity of seal meat has not been investigated. Read more on this subject in chapter 5, p. 135.

Skins purchased by Grønlands Skindindhandling (Greenland Fur Traders), 1981–2000.

Year	Qty. skins	Year	Qty. skins
1981	55,663	1992	69,140
1982	55,211	1993	52,056
1983	47,842	1994	60,339
1984	52,514	1995	53,211
1985	50,526	1996	76,267
1986	? no data	1997	73,971
1987	? no data	1998	83,752
1988	57,545	1999	106,100
1989	45,038	2000	102,700
1990	53,471	2001	?
1991	64,530		

Source: *staff info., Grønlands Skindindhandling 2001.*

Individual species

Ringed Seal →?

Ringed Seals are found in all sea areas off Greenland. Most prevalent in Northwest and East Greenland where most kills occur.

Steady annual increases in Ringed Seal kills from approx. 35,000 animals in 1954 to the current level of 75,000–90,000 have been recorded. As stocks levels show no signs of decline, this increasing level of kills is still regarded as 'probably sustainable'. Furthermore, Greenland kills primarily consist of males and very young animals, and as a result the species is assumed to be safe from any possible over exploitation because of large population numbers, and the wide distribution of the species throughout most of the Arctic region.

About half the total kill is made during winter months using nets deployed under the ice that drown the animals. Seal meat is used both as human and dog food. Sealskins are purchased with the support of massive Government subsidies and as a result, Ringed Seals are still the main source of incomes for numerous settlements.

There are no kill restrictions apart from local regulations that are mostly designed to protect sites which seals frequent in summer. Additionally, there are general protection regulations operating in the North and Northeast Greenland National Park and in the Melville Bay Wildlife Reserve.

Harbour Seal ↓

Found in all inhabited areas of Greenland, where regular hunting of the species occurred during the first half of the twentieth century with annual kills of about 1,000 animals. In recent years the annual Harbour Seal kill has fallen to less than 300.

Nowadays the species is very rare and has been driven from many of its former sites. For instance, as late as the 1960s there were sightings of several hundred seals on land in the Søndre Strømfjord delta, but today the animals have all but vanished. Intensive monitoring of the area with video cameras during the period 1995–97 yielded sightings of a mere seven Harbour Seals.

Because the species is so rare Harbour Seals are only killed occasionally today. Even modest annual kills of less than 300 animals recorded by *Piniarneq* are probably too high because Ringed Seals are often mistakenly counted as Harbour Seals. For the years 1993–95 Grønlands Skindindhandling (Greenland Fur Traders) only purchased 13, 38 and 33 Harbour Seal skins respectively.

In the traditional West Greenland national costume Harbour Seal fur is used to make 'ladies trousers', but nowadays sealskins have to be imported from countries such as Iceland to keep up with the demand in Greenland.

Adult Harbour Seals are the only protected seal species in Greenland. Hunting is banned between 1 May and 1 October, which is when the seals come ashore to give birth and moult.

Additionally, old familiar haul-out sites in the Paamiut/Frederikshåb and Qaqortoq/Julianehåb municipalities are protected against hunting and disturbance. However, it is highly unlikely that these local regulations are respected, or even enforced.

Increased hunting, and boat traffic, together with inadvertent drowning of seals in trout and Salmon nets are presumed to be some of the reasons for the prolonged decline.

Bearded Seal →?

Bearded Seals are hunted in all inhabited areas of Greenland, but numbers are low everywhere. Although most sightings are of lone animals the species is evenly distributed throughout most of the Arctic region.

Between 1954 and 1985 kill statistics showed the annual catch as 500–1,000 seals, but according to official *Piniarneq 2001* statistics 1,800–2,350 animals are killed annually. There are no restrictions for Bearded Seal kills in Greenland and the species can be hunted all year round.

Researchers only have limited information on Bearded Seal stocks in Greenland. However, extensive and even distribution of the species throughout most of the Arctic region is assumed to be a 'buffer' against over-exploitation.

Harp Seal ↑

Killed in large numbers in all inhabited areas in Greenland. Most hunting occurs during the summer when large numbers of Harp Seals arrive in Southwest Greenland during May and June before fanning out along coastlines to the north. Harp Seals leave these northern areas in late autumn and mostly return to their breeding grounds in Newfoundland and Jan Mayen.

Harp Seals do not breed in Greenland territorial waters – although the scientific name *Phoca groenlandica* gives the impression that they might. Nevertheless Greenland's hunters were obviously affected by boycott campaigns against the February–March mass slaughter of newborn pups on the pack ice around Newfoundland. Sealskin sales from Greenland were also hit by EU import restrictions, despite the fact that the '*Council Directive 83/129/EEC of 28 March 1983 concerning the importation into Member States of skins of certain seal pups and products derived therefrom*' specifically stated that: '*This Directive shall only apply to products not resulting from traditional hunting by the Inuit people.*'

Harp Seal kills have fluctuated widely in the past. In the 1940s and beginning of the 1950s more than 20,000 Harp Seals were traded annually according to hunting statistics. But numbers fell to 6,000–7,000 by the end of the 1960s. Thereafter total kills increased steadily to 15,000–20,000 by the start of the 1980s.

Reliable statistics are unavailable for the period following, but, according to *Piniarneq 2001,* numbers have been increasing continually with 82,491 kills recorded in 1998. Today, kills – and hunters' incomes – are many times greater than for the period prior to the start of the highly controversial anti-sealskin campaigns. Two thirds of all skins landed are sold to Grønlands Skindindhandling (Greenland Fur Traders).

Harp Seal hunting in Greenland is totally unrestricted, and there are no specific regulations applying to the management of stocks. Since 1999 there have been many reports of thousands of seal carcasses being dumped at sea, simply because far more animals are killed than can possibly be eaten. Hunting circles are very aware that the current practice of throwing away such large quantities of seal meat can trigger off a negative reaction from abroad. Nevertheless seals continue to be killed without their meat being used.

Latest research estimates indicate that the birth of pups on the pack ice off Newfoundland has increased from about 580,000 pups in 1990 to 700,000 in 1994. This corresponds to a total population of nearly five million Harp Seals. The population situation around Jan Mayen is less well documented. Birth numbers are much lower at around 60,000 pups per year, corresponding to 300,000 adult Harp Seals. No one knows whether this population is stable, increasing or declining.

In 1996, Canada revived commercial hunting in earnest setting an annual quota of 275,000 Harp Seals for 1997, 1998 and 1999. This level of kills is officially regarded as sustainable, but researchers from the *International Marine Mammal Association* IMMA, allege that in reality somewhere between two and six times more Harp Seals are killed than can be supported by the population. This quota level is expected to stabilise stocks at around current levels according to the Canadian Government's scientific advisors.

Hooded Seal ↑

Killed in all inhabited areas of Greenland, though rarely in North and Northeast Greenland. Hooded Seals are generally shot from dinghies or small motorboats with hunting taking place mainly from April–June in West Greenland, and almost always in the month of July in East Greenland.

In former times adult sealskin were used in the construction of *umiaks* and *kayaks*. Nowadays, pelts from young animals are used in the fur trade.

Absolutely no restrictions apply to the hunting of Hooded Seals in Greenland.

Approximately 1,200 animals were killed annually around 1960. By 1985 numbers had increased to 5,000–6,000 seals. According to figures published in *Piniarneq 2001,* somewhere between 7,000–10,000 Hooded Seals were killed annually in the 1990s.

Hooded Seals establish breeding sites on the pack ice off Newfoundland, in the middle of the Davis Strait, and around Jan Mayen. The total number of Hooded Seal pups born in Northwest Atlantic sites is currently estimated to be at least 84,000 pups. This corresponds to a total population of about 350,000 seals. The exact Hooded Seal population at Jan Mayen is not known, but this has only limited impact on Greenland kills.

Despite increasing hunting pressure in Greenland, researchers estimate that the population is rising. This increase may well be explained by the fact that commercial hunting of Hooded Seals in Canada has been at a standstill since the start of the 1980s. The

1996–97 Canadian quota was set at 8,000 animals. A quota of 10,000 seals was allocated for 1998.

Walrus *(Odobenus rosmarus rosmarus)* ↓

Walrus populations have sharply declined throughout Greenland due to intense hunting pressures. Despite the reduction in stocks 300–600 animals continue to be killed every year. More animals (25–30 per cent) die, or are lost at sea from wounds received.

Hunters particularly target large, adult animals (larger tusks and more meat), and this poses a particular threat to the population. Meat, blubber and hide are mainly used for dog food, while walrus tusk-bearing skulls are sold to tourists, or used for craft articles and tools. In recent years repeated finds have been made of slaughtered carcass remains, where only the Walrus's tusk-bearing head had been removed.

Killing Walruses is the preserve of professional hunters, but there are no quota restrictions.

Walruses are protected all year round in West Greenland south of latitude 66°N (halfway between Sisimiut and Maniitsoq). However, except for certain periodic restrictions traditional hunting is permitted in the municipalities of Upernavik, Qaanaaq/Thule, and Illoqqortoormiut/Scoresbysund.

Walruses are included in both the CITES and Bern Convention articles, which means that in the EU, any trade in Walrus products is subject to tight import controls.

Walruses had already been driven away from all their West Greenland haul-out sites in the first half of the twentieth century, though the species still overwinters in two offshore areas. In those days Greenlanders did most of the hunting – encouraged by financial inducements from the Royal Greenland Trade Department (KGH).

Although protected since 1956, a number of adult females have still been illegally killed in West Greenland during the close season. Since the 1960s, the increasing use of dinghies with high-powered engines has subjected Walruses to further hunting pressure. In 1995

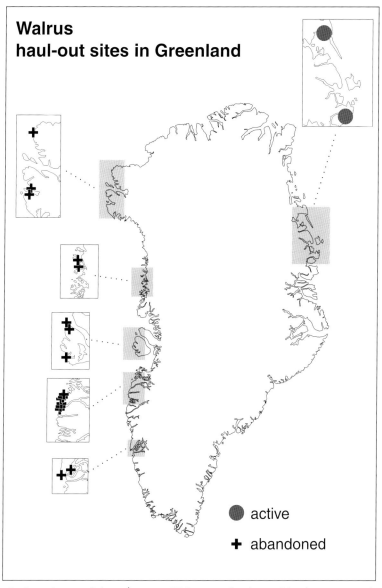

Walrus haul-out sites in Greenland

active

abandoned

In the early part of the 20th century Walruses used at least 16 haul-out sites on the west coast from Nuuk/Godthåb up to Avanersuaq. Today Walruses have been forced to abandon all terrestrial sites in Greenland except two haul-out sites in the North and Northeast Greenland Nationalpark. These changes have been caused by increased hunting. Source: *Born et al. (1994, 1995).*

international researchers estimated the population size to be 1,500–4,000 animals, but counts made from aircraft for the period 1981–1993 indicate that numbers in the central part of West Greenland are lower than this, with stocks generally in decline.

The size of the population in the *Nordvand* area off Avanersuaq is virtually unknown, but over-exploitation of stocks cannot be ruled out. Previous population size guesstimates of 7,500–19,000 animals now look highly inflated. There are no recorded sightings from the area to indicate that a population of this size exists.

Walruses were intensively hunted in East Greenland up to the middle of the last century. Scientific expeditions, and Danish and Norwegian hunters stationed in Greenland all took part in regular massacres of Walruses. Today Greenland's only two remaining onshore haul-out sites are found in the North and Northeast Greenland National Park, where Walruses have been unconditionally protected since 1956. The population is estimated to comprise 500–1,000 animals.

According to researchers, quotas have been necessary for a long time. Without them Walrus populations are expected to decline. As early as 1995 NAMMCO recommended that Greenland should attempt to prevent the decline of Walrus populations. In the autumn of 2000 the Greenland Home Rule Government committed itself in principle to tighten Walrus hunting regulations with quotas and quota allocations along the same lines as Beluga and Narwhal catches (see p. 89).

Whales

Beluga *(Delphinapterus leucas)* ↓

The prevalence of Belugas around West Greenland has altered radically over the past 70–90 years. Previously, the species migrated as far south as Qaqortoq/Julianehåb, where Belugas were caught prior to 1900. Today, Belugas are seldom seen south of Maniitsoq/Sukkertoppen. Belugas are rarely sighted or caught in East Greenland waters.

Up to about 1930 the greatest numbers of whales were caught in waters around South Greenland. During the 1920s the Royal Greenland Trade Department (KGH) organized large-scale whaling operations using KGH owned motorboats. At that time KGH exported both blubber and *mattak* to Europe where, amongst other things, the *mattak* was tanned and used in the production of shoes. Undoubtedly, commercial whaling on this scale hastened the demise of numerous local whale populations.

Since then kills have been greatest during autumn months around Upernavik, and off the Sisimiut/Holsteinsborg coasts during the spring. Large numbers of Belugas were killed in years when conditions were especially favourable, for example: 1,874 whales in 1954, 1,259 in 1968 and 1,524 in 1970. More than 1,000 whales were killed annually as recently as 1981 and 1990. Since 1975 official kill figures have gradually become less accurate. In the same period the value of *mattak* has increased.

Belugas are shot and killed with rifles in different hunting circumstances: Hunting in open water, along ice edges, 'sassat' (ice entrapments), and also with nets. Kills are not subject to quotas and both professional and leisure hunters are allowed to hunt Belugas. However, some conditions need to be fulfilled with regard to types of weapons and boats that are deployed.

The species is protected under the CITES convention. Anyone wishing to export Beluga products needs permission from the Greenland Home Rule Government.

Currently, 700 Beluga kills are recorded annually. Without any doubt this figure is too high – i.e. kill levels are not sustainable. Censuses also show that the Beluga population off West Greenland has declined by over 50 per cent since 1980. The Greenland Institute of Natural Resources has warned that there is a serious risk of Belugas vanishing from West Greenland waters during the next twenty years if catches continue at current levels. Biologists have made it clear that the maximum sustainable annual Beluga catch should be less than 100.

Estimated Beluga population based on aerial surveys.

Year	1982	1994	1999
No. Belugas	19,689	10,230	7,941

Note: Large schools of Belugas comprising fifty or more animals were a common sight during the 1981–82 census. In contrast, censuses in the 1990s recorded that schools generally only consisted of ten or less animals, and also the presence of many lone Belugas. Source: *Hvidbog om Hvidhvaler. Grønlands Naturinstitut, 2001.*

The trend since the 1980s is for kills to be made further and further to the north. Simultaneously, hunting has been 'industrialised' with shore-based facilities and factory fishing ships assisting the process. As recently as 1999 NuKa A/S (a Greenland Home Rule owned company) put a factory ship into service in the Upernavik region, and the company is also building a production facility in Upernavik municipality specifically designed to receive *mattak*. These investments are expected to further stimulate hunting activity.

The much sought after *mattak* (whale skin with subcutaneous blubber) is a popular delicacy and is purchased for resale in south-western Greenland. Frozen *mattak* can be bought in Nuuk/Godthåb supermarkets amongst other places. According to Statistics Greenland, 19.7 tons of Beluga *mattak* was purchased in 1998. Greenlanders also use the meat, but there have been some incidents over recent years when valuable *mattak* was landed while whale carcasses were left rotting on the ice.

On several occasions during the 1990s JCCM (Canada-Greenland Joint Commission for the Conservation and Management of Narwhal and Beluga) has strongly recommended that Greenland reduces Beluga kills. In June 2000, NAMMCO (North Atlantic Marine Mammal Commission), which has Norway, Iceland, the Faroe Islands and Greenland as members, similarly recommended that annual kills be limited to 100 whales. NAMMCO also recommended that this quota be proportionately distributed in relation to current kills. To safeguard the reproduction of the species Belugas should also be protected at specific times of the year with additional protection for females and calves.

In the autumn of 2000 the Greenland Home Rule Government committed itself in principle to introduce a system of quotas covering kills of Belugas and Narwhals with effect from August 2001. This decision triggered off a storm of protests from the professional hunters' trade union KNAPK, the Greenland Municipal Federation KANUKOKA, and the organisation representing leisure hunters TPAK. The reactions from KNAPK were particularly vehement and the organisation accused biologists at JCCM, NAMMCO and the Greenland Institute of Natural Resources of lying.

The protests worked: In May 2001 the Ministry of Industry announced its intention to postpone a decision on quotas until the spring of 2002.

Narwhal (*Monodon monoceros*) →?

Occurs in spring and winter along the West Greenland coasts and is specially numerous in Disko Bay. Seldom found south of Aasiaat/Egedesminde. Particularly common during the summer in the Avanersuaq municipality and Melville Bay areas. Narwhals are common in Upernavik and Uummannaq waters during autumn months.

Found off East Greenland from May to November within major fiord systems including Kangertiitivaq/Scoresby Sund. Narwhals spend the winter at the mouths of these fiords.

Narwhal *mattak* (whale skin with subcutaneous blubber) is a favourite delicacy similar to Beluga *mattak*. Narwhal meat is used locally or exported to townships in southwest Greenland, where Narwhals do not occur. Some of the meat is used for dog food. Narwhal tusks are traded or sold locally and turned into handicraft products.

Narwhals are protected under the CITES Convention and the Narwhal tusk trade is regulated. The EU has tightened CITES regulations by banning all imports of Narwhal tusks. However, imports to Denmark from Greenland are not covered allowing these products to be re-exported within the EU.

No quotas exist, and Narwhals can be hunted by anybody holding a professional or leisure permit. There are however some limitations in respect of weapon types and transport means used for hunting, etc.

Narwhal kills 1993–1999.

Year	1993	1994	1995	1996	1997	1998	1999*
Total kills	633	881	554	738	797	822	482

* Only includes kills from January to September. Source: *Piniarneq 2001, Greenland Institute of Natural Resources.*

Narwhals are regularly hunted in the Avanersuaq municipality, where an estimated 200–300 animals are killed every year. In Uummannaq annual kills vary between 100–300 animals, but has sometimes climbed to 1,000 animals. In addition Narwhals are killed in Upernavik and the Disko Bay areas, though usually in considerably fewer numbers.

At least 80 East Greenland Narwhals are estimated to have been killed during the period 1981–90.

It is likely that considerably more Narwhals are killed than are reported as it is common knowledge that professional hunters from Avanersuaq often fail to register kills or directly boycott the reporting process. No one really knows the actual size of the population/stocks, or the number of kills, and this includes wounded Narwhals that are lost at sea. As a result there is no information about whether present exploitation is sustainable in the long term.

However, according to NAMMCO there is reason to suppose that Narwhals are killed at a sustainable level. The Narwhal's status is currently under revue at NAMMCO. It is expected that restrictions will be placed on Narwhal kills, even though information about population sizes, kill quantities and other related data is highly inadequate. These measures are deemed necessary in response to fears that Narwhal populations will otherwise be subjected to increasing collateral pressure following the implementation of Beluga kill restrictions.

In the autumn of 2000 the Greenland Home Rule Government committed itself in principle to introduce quotas from Augsut 2001 to coincide with the introduction of Beluga quotas. In May 2001 the Ministry of Industry announced its intention to postpone a decision on quotas until the spring of 2002.

Minke Whale *(Balaenoptera acutorostrata)* →?

Found along the entire West Greenland coastline in sheltered waters, as well as open sea areas. In recent years the Minke Whales have occurred closer to the coast and with greater numbers off Southwest Greenland. In East Greenland Minke Whales are found near the coasts of Tasiilaq/Ammassalik and Illoqqortoormiut/Scoresbysund.

Off *West Greenland*, Minke Whales are thought to belong to a separate stock. It is not known whether numbers in this area are on the increase, in balance or declining. Greenland whalers have killed Minke Whales for 50 years but despite this fact there is no information as to where West Greenland's Minke Whales spend the winter. Based on aerial censuses in 1993, Minke Whale populations are estimated to be somewhere between 2,400–16,900 animals.

Ostensibly Minke Whales around *East Greenland* belong to the Icelandic population, though scientific research has not been able to confirm this assumption. Censuses conducted in Iceland in 1987 and 1989 resulted in population estimates of between 21,600–31,400 Minke Whales in the central Atlantic area. There is no separate estimate for Southeast Greenland and no information is available on population trends. As a result it is not possible to conclude whether present kill levels have negative consequences.

Despite the fact that Minke Whales are protected under the CITES Convention, the International Whaling Commission (IWC) has granted Greenland a quota under the heading of 'aboriginal subsistence hunting'. This phrase is defined as 'hunting by aboriginal people for the maintenance of cultural and nutritional needs', but, amongst other conditions, the commercial export of meat from kills is prohibited.

The 1995–97 three-year quota for West Greenland totalled 465 Minke Whales, or 155 per year. In East Greenland the quota was set at 12 animals per year. This large difference between the two quotas can be seen as an expression of the fact that the biggest quota was granted to areas with most inhabitants. Quota sizes in no way reflect the locations where Minke Whale stocks are best able to withstand the heavier exploitation.

In 1996 168 Minke Whales were reportedly killed in West Greenland, of which 109 were killed with harpoon canons, 50 by rifle (!), 1 illegally, 4 wounded and lost and 4 caught in nets. In East Greenland that same year the entire quota of 12 Minke Whales was taken up. As these figures show hunters frequently use rifles to kill Minke Whales by pursuing whales in small dinghies until they successfully kill the animal. This type of collective hunting often lasts for hours and no one can deny that these hunting methods are unacceptable in terms of animal welfare.

Greenland is the only country in the world permitted by the International Whaling Commission to kill part of its Minke Whale quota with rifles, though there is good reason to be sceptical about official figures. The Greenland fishing newspaper *Aalisartoq*, investigated the underlying catch figures from 1997, where harpoon grenades reportedly killed 106 Minke Whales. In fact, journalists discovered that only twenty grenades were actually sold that year. In the case of Fin Whales only six grenades were sold, even though a total of 11 Fin Whales were killed in 1997. The paper concluded that considerable illegal whaling was taking place using rifles and 'cold' harpoons. During this period Greenland's Home Rule Government paid a grant of DKK 3,400 for every harpoon grenade sold.

The International Whaling Commission set an annual quota of 175 Minke Whales for West Greenland and 12 for East Greenland for the five-year period between 1998–2002. If quotas are not fully used in any given year, a small element of the unused quota can be transferred to the following year.

In January 2001, KNAPK, the organisation representing fishermen and hunters, called on the Greenland Home Rule Government to work towards the development of possibilities for the commercial export of Minke Whale meat and blubber. The Ministry of Industry considers the introduction of commercial whaling in Greenland to be 'a difficult and complicated affair'. Greenland would undoubtedly be forced to give up its present status as 'an aboriginal people', along with the (aboriginal subsistence hunting) right to kill animals that are otherwise protected across most of the world.

Fin Whale *(Balaenoptera physalus)* →?

Found around West Greenland from Nunap Isua/Kap Farvel to Upernavik, on fishing banks and around inshore waters, where these large mammals are a popular attraction for tourists and locals. Around East Greenland Fin Whales are mostly found east of the drift ice belt.

There is no information as to whether Fin Whales around West Greenland are on the increase, stable or declining. The population is estimated at somewhere between 520 and 2,100 animals, but this estimate is based on censuses from as far back as 1987–89. Also it is not known whether Fin Whales around West Greenland belong to a separate stock. If this is true, then there is reason for concern about the current level of kills.

Although Fin Whales are protected under the CITES Convention, the International Whaling Commission (IWC) has granted Greenland a quota under the heading of 'aboriginal subsistence hunting'. This phrase is defined as 'hunting by aboriginal people for the maintenance of cultural and nutritional needs', but, amongst other conditions, the commercial export of meat from kills is prohibited.

Despite the lack of information about Fin Whales in Greenland's waters, annual kills have been constantly rising. In 1978 the quota was set at 4 Fin Whales. In 1993 the quota was increased to 21 animals. Fin Whale quotas have been fixed at nineteen whales per year for 1998–2002. Hitherto, professional hunters have been unable to fully utilise the quota (see kill figures below). According to KNAPK, this has been due to difficulties in finding what the organisation describes as 'purchasing opportunities' – in other words how to sell the meat. Current legislation stipulates that any whale meat from Fin Whales must be utilised 100 per cent.

It is illegal to kill Fin Whales less than 15.2 metres long and this rule also applies to females with calves. Wounded whales that get away or are lost at sea are not counted in quotas. Fin Whales are not hunted in East Greenland.

Fin Whale kills 1988–2000.

Year	1988	1989	1990	1991	1992	1993	1994	1995	1996	1997	1998	1999	2000
Kills	9	10	20	18	22	20	24	12	19	14	9	7	6

Source: *Greenland Institute of Natural Resources.*

Ostensibly only persons with a professional hunting permit can apply for a license to kill Fin Whales. Whales have to be killed using harpoon guns mounted on larger vessels and these also have to be equipped with line or trawl capstans. Shooting Fin Whales with rifles or the use of 'cold' harpoons is prohibited, but it happens anyway. The disparity between the numbers of harpoon grenades sold and whales actually killed (see also p. 92 on Minke Whales) substantiates this. In recent years tourists have also provided accounts of Fin Whales being shot at for hours in attempts by locals to kill these huge mammals.

Terrestrial mammals

The Ministry of Industry manages stocks of Caribou and Muskox by fixing annual quotas and issuing permits. These are based on population developments monitored on a year-to-year basis. Hunting Caribou is extremely popular and nearly everyone tries to get a share of these annual quotas. In July 2000 the Greenland Home Rule Government was forced to raise the age limit for leisure hunters applying for Caribou quotas from 12 to 16 years, so as to limit the number of children that applied for a share of these quotas.

Caribou *(Rangifer tarandus groenlandicus)* ↑

Found on the west coast of Greenland and in Inglefield Land north of Qaanaaq. Caribous are most numerous in the areas around

Nuuk/Godthåb, Maniitsoq/Sukkertoppen and Sisimiut/Holsteinsborg.

Caribou numbers are known to fluctuate widely all over the world. These changes to population numbers are assumed to be due to interactions between climatic changes, excessive grazing, natural predators and hunting pressures. Previously, fluctuations in caribou kills meant that local caribou populations in Greenland correspondingly increased or decreased, but nowadays hunting is regulated by quotas.

Caribou hunting peaked between 1970–76, when the number of officially recorded kills in West Greenland rose to between 10,000 and 17,000 animals. In 1990 estimates put the number of Caribou in West Greenland at 20,000, but figures from 1993 showed a declining population of 10,000 animals. On the assumption that the decline was caused by excessive hunting Caribou were unconditionally protected in 1993 and 1994. Following censuses in 1995 and 1996 the Caribou population was estimated to be between 17,600 and 20,000 animals. Hunting recommenced in 1995, but annual quotas have varied in line with local stocks.

Improved census methods in 1999–2001 have resulted in a further update of Caribou population numbers. The increase in numbers is so dramatic that the only possible explanation is that the previous 1993–96 censuses wildly underestimated stock sizes. An estimated 43,143 Caribou were counted following a March 2000 helicopter census of stocks in only the northern regions. By contrast 1996 estimates indicated the presence of only 10,900 animals!

And Caribou stocks continue to grow. The Greenland Institute of Natural Resources estimated that the total population has mushroomed to 140,000 animals in 2001. These revised population figures have led to a dramatic increase in quotas, which are hardly likely to be utilised in full. The production company NuKa A/S has directly protested against these high quotas, as the company has no capacity to process such large quantities of meat.

Hunting quotas for Caribou in West Greenland 1995–2001.

1995	1996	1997	1998	1999	2000	2001
2,000	2,600	3,111	3,680	4,100	13,260	24,300

Source: *Greenland Institute of Natural Resources.*

Caribou quotas require permits that specify: How many animals can be killed, where Caribou can be hunted, and during which periods. Leisure hunting applicants must be over 16 years old. Hunters are duty bound to provide detailed information about the hunt and the number of animals killed. Additionally, hunters are required to either eat all the meat on site or carry it with them. Selling Caribou meat is the preserve of professional hunters.

Muskox *(Ovibus moschatus)* ↑

Naturally distributed populations of Muskox cover Northeast and East Greenland as far south as Illoqqortoormiut/Scoresbysund. Muskoxen were relocated from these areas to a number of locations in Southwest, West and Northwest Greenland, which nowadays all boast well-established populations.

The original population probably existed as three sub-groups, which were on the increase during the first half of the 20th century. The number of Muskoxen in North and Northeast Greenland was estimated at between 9,500 and 12,500 animals in 1990. Estimating the effects of exploitation is difficult because there is no information about numbers of kills and the impact of hunting.

Muskoxen are protected in the North and Northeast Greenland National Park, which contains 95 per cent of the original population. However, during Polar Bear hunting trips hunters are allowed to kill Muskoxen in the Park area as food for sledge dogs.

Stocks of animals that were relocated to the west coast seem in all cases to be on the increase or stable. The first Muskox relocations occurred between 1961–65 when 27 Muskoxen from Northeast Greenland were set free in an area near Kangerlussuaq/Søndre Strømfjord. This small herd had grown to a population of 1,261 animals by

1987, and hunting of these animals started that same year. 1993 estimates put the population at approx. 4,000 animals. Just two years later in 1995, stocks in the area had fallen to 2,500–3,000 animals. Sightings in spring 2000 recorded 4,235 oxen in the region. Between 1987–1997 a total of 4,500–5,000 Muskoxen were killed, an average of nearly 500 per year.

The Muskox quota for 2001 was raised from 880 to 1,200 animals on the grounds that stocks continue to grow. Coinciding with this quota increase an abattoir with a capacity to process 20 animals per day has been set up in Kangerlussuaq/Søndre Strømfjord – amongst other things with an eye on exports to Europe. However, the abattoir has been plagued by major quality control problems. A ton of meat had to be condemned in 2001 because carcasses either had too many gun shot wounds, or had rotted on their way (by dog sledge) to the slaughterhouse. A total of 16 tons of meat was reportedly condemned for similar reasons in 2000.

In addition a modest number of animals are killed in the municipality of Ivituut where the 15 Muskoxen released in 1987 have multiplied over the intervening ten years to a population of about 150 animals. All other populations that were released are still protected against hunting.

Muskoxen were released in West Greenland in an experiment designed to increase hunting opportunities for professional hunters, and to establish the foundations of a commercial tourist trophy-hunting business. Hunting is subject to quotas and persons holding professional and leisure hunting licenses can apply for permits. Leisure hunters have to be at least 16 years old when applying. Hunters are duty bound to provide detailed information about the hunt and the number of animals killed. Additionally, hunters are required to either store all the meat and hide, or carry it with them.

Shrimps, Bivalves and Crabs

The Ministry of Industry is responsible for managing catches of shellfish and bivalves. Exploitation of Deep Sea Shrimp, which is based on monitored quotas, seems to be taking place at a sustainable level today. Quotas are fixed on the basis of comprehensive monitoring of shrimp stock sizes. It is however worth noting that the significant decline in catches between 1992–98 may indicate that exploitation is at a maximum.

Even though Greenland has in-depth experience in shrimp resources' management, recent years have witnessed increased exploitation of Scallops and Crabs. True enough, catches are officially based on quotas but these do not follow the actual advice of biologists. Several local stocks of both Scallops and Crabs have already been fished out. Yields are generally on the decline in relation to the effort deployed – a situation that indicates over exploitation.

Deep Sea Shrimp *(Pandalus borealis)* ↑

Deep Sea Shrimps are Greenland's most financially significant species. Greenland exported frozen shrimps to a value of DKK 1.15 billion in 1998 – a figure that corresponds to 67 percent of the country's total export income. Shrimp fisheries also generate substantial employment, both in the fishing operation itself and at onshore processing plants.

After two decades of explosive growth in the shrimp fisheries' sector, catches of Deep Sea Shrimp in Greenland's territorial waters fell in 1992, though shrimp stocks seem to be on the increase again after 1997.

Up to the start of the 1970s the annual *West Greenland* shrimp fishery was less than 10,000 tons, mostly caught by small fishing boats operating in sheltered waters. After 1969 deep sea fishing by larger trawlers resulted in rapid increases in catches with 43,000 tons recorded as early as 1976. Tonnages continued to rise and peaked at a record 80,000 tons in 1992. In 1996 the total catch had fallen back to approx. 67,000 tons.

The annual shrimp quota for 1999–2000 was 71,000 tons, but for 2001 scientists recommended a maximum TAC (Total Annual Catch) of 85,000 tons. However, the Greenland Home Rule Government adopted a cautious strategy and fixed the quota at 82,000 tons.

Shrimp fishing off *East Greenland* first began in 1978, and catches increased dramatically from 4,000 tons in 1983 to 11,000 tons in 1988. Since then catches have fallen consistently, plummeting to only 4,000 tons in 1995. Quotas also now apply to East Greenland with 10,600 tons allocated for each of the years 1999–2001. The 2001 quota is 1,000 tons greater than the level recommended by scientists.

Shrimp fishing from large trawlers has been subject to quotas ever since 1977, and quota restrictions have been implemented for smaller fishing vessels from 1996. Quotas can be freely traded, though only between similar types of vessels. Shrimp fisheries are also regulated by enforcing the use of a minimum 40 mm mesh size for trawls. To protect Redfish spawning grounds an area along the east coast is completely off limits to shrimp fisheries.

Shrimp trawlers operate with bottom trawls, where two giant trawl boards expand a net bag behind the ship. This net bag is fitted with heavy weights enabling the bag to drag over the seabed. The technology produces considerable mechanical disturbance of the sea floor, and destroys all fauna in its path. Other species such as bivalves, which exist by filtering water, can be negatively affected by these swirls of seabed debris. Finally this mechanical mixing of the soft muddy sea floor results in alterations of the circulation velocity of both organic and non-organic matter. No one knows the scale of these changes, or how much sea floor fauna is destroyed.

In the early days the use of bottom trawls with small mesh sizes was responsible for large secondary catches of small Greenland Halibut, Redfish and Polar Cod, which had no market value. Problems of wasted catches of this type have been less in recent years, though this is most likely due to the sharp decline in many seabed fish species that are now only found in juvenile sizes in shrimp fishing areas. The obligatory use of sorting grates in shrimp trawls should help reduce secondary catches.

Scallop *(Chlamys islandica)* ↓

Scallops are common along the entire western coastline of Greenland up to Qaanaaq/Thule. Only sporadically found on the east coast.

Scallop fishing is based on a permit system and catches for individual Scallop beds have been subject to quotas since the end of the 1980s. Most years, these quotas, which are fixed by the Greenland Home Rule Government, have been higher than those recommended by biologists. In 1994 the Nuuk beds were re-evaluated, and surveys showed that biomass had halved since 1988 – in other words the total amount of Scallops (in tons) in these beds had fallen to 50 per cent of previous levels after six years of over fishing.

In 1995 a transplanting experiment was launched in the Nuuk area. The aim was to re-establish Scallop beds destroyed by over fishing. Although Scallops adapted reasonably well to transplantation, mortality rates of juvenile Scallops were high, and growth rates of adult Scallops so low, that the authorities were forced to conclude that: '*In view of the costs connected with implementing such a project, Scallop transplantation on a major scale in Nuuk would be economically unfeasible.*'

Total annual catches have been stable for a long time at around 2,000 tons, but fishery logbooks report declining catch rates in all sectors (catch per trip). There is little doubt that Scallop beds are generally over fished.

Scallop fishing is carried out by medium sized fishing vessels of 100–200 tons. A heavy iron scraper system weighing up to several tons is used to scrape up the Scallops. This leaves the sea floor heavily churned up and uneven. Large boulders are frequently lifted out of the sediment and in all probability sea floor fauna is destroyed over a wide area. The process throws up a thick cloud of sediment in the water and this can have a negative effect on Scallops and other fixed shellfish, as the large quantities of clay or mud can block their gills.

Scallop fishing is regarded as one of the reasons why the large 380 km² Aqajarua/Mudderbugten in Disko Bay has ceased to be important as a moulting site for the entire Canada-Greenland population of King Eiders. See p. 71 for further details.

Snow Crab *(Chionoecetes opilio)* ↓

Only found along the west coast of Greenland. Fishing for Snow Crabs started in sheltered waters in 1992. Open sea Crab fishing began in earnest in 1999.

The coastal fishery started in Disko Bay and at Sisimiut/Holsteinsborg, and has since spread to other areas along the west coast. Catches have varied considerably from year to year, but total catches have generally been growing.

There is little information about the extent or the locations of the fishery because fishermen are not required to record catch statistics of their commercial fishing activities. Crab stock figures are incomplete and only cover the most recent years. Because of this lack of data, both Crab fishermen and biologists are uneasy about the growing incidence of Crab fishing.

Crab purchases in tons from inshore fisheries, 1995–2000.

1995	1996	1997	1998	1999	2000*
997	739	3,214	2,094	2,978	3,333

* Catch figures are provisional and do not cover the entire year. Source: *Greenland Institute of Natural Resources.*

Against the advice of biologists, Greenland's Home Rule Government voted in favour of a substantial inshore Crab fishing quota increase to 17,000 tons in 2001. This was more than double the quota of the previous year, and contrary to the advice from the Greenland Institute of Natural Resources, which had recommended a total all-sector sheltered water catch of maximum 5,000 tons.

But to even the balance the Home Rule Government reduced the quota for open sea fishing from 25,000 tons to 17,000 tons. No accurate biological information is available for open sea Crab populations and biologists are unable to advise on sustainable catch levels. But according to a Crab fisheries representative open sea fishing stocks could easily be destroyed within the next five years.

In 2001 a fleet of 11 ocean-going trawlers was involved in open sea Crab fishing operations. There is also fierce competition from Norwegian and Canadian fishermen.

Crab purchases in tons from open sea fishing, 1999–2000.

1999	2000*
2,004	2,255

* Catch figures are provisional and do not cover the entire year. Source: *Greenland Institute of Natural Resources*

Crab fishing in sheltered waters is carried out using baited Crab pots. Pots are rigged to a line and numbers vary from just a few to as many as 50. The fishery is purely commercial with Crabs sold to processing plants or factory fishing ships.

At the moment there are no problems with secondary catches of other species, apart from several instances in recent years of Humpback Whales entangled in Crab pot lines, where whales either drowned or had to be destroyed. Ten Humpback Whales reportedly died like this in 2000, but confirmation of these reports has not been possible despite repeated requests to the Ministry of Industry in Nuuk/Godthåb.

The use of Crab pots has no negative effects on actual ocean habitats.

Fish

Today, all commercial fish stocks around Greenland are over fished with scientists advising that a long list of species should not be caught. Currently, the management of fish stocks around Greenland is based on annual quotas that are fixed after consultation with ICES

(*International Council for Exploration of the Sea*) and NAFO (*Northwest Atlantic Fisheries Organization*).

During the last century the reduction in stocks of several species was so great that nowadays they have no economic importance. Two good examples of this trend are Cod and Atlantic Salmon that were all but exterminated in the 1970s.

But the classic example is the Atlantic Halibut (*Hippoglossus hippoglossus)*, where stocks were depleted as early as around 1930. Up to then Atlantic Halibut in Greenland waters existed in far greater numbers, and individual fish reached remarkable sizes of up to 250 cm and weights of nearly 300 kilos.

The Atlantic Halibut fishery in the late 1920s and early 1930s was big business with catches peaking in 1929 at nearly 7,000 tons. Most Halibut were caught by foreign vessels using line fishing techniques.

Catches were 1,000 to 2,000 tons annually in the 1950s, but by the early 1970s catches had fallen to under 500 tons. By 1989 the catch had fallen still further to about 200 tons and today the Atlantic Halibut fishing bonanza is definitely over. In 1997 a mere 22 tons of small Atlantic Halibut were landed, but these were only secondary catches from fishing for other species.

Greenland Halibut (*Reinhardtius hippoglossoides*) ↓

In former times, the Greenland Halibut was an important food element in Greenland households – both for human consumption, and as dog food. Today, the species is only fished commercially and is Greenland's next most important export commodity after Deep Sea Shrimps.

There has been a Greenland Halibut fishery around Ilulissat/Jakobshavn since the start of the last century. Up until the 1960s catches were between 3–400 tons annually. Catch figures of Greenland Halibut shot up to about 1,000 tons a year during the 1960s. Since the 1980s this figure has rocketed. Between 15,000 and 20,000 tons are now caught annually in the fiord areas between Disko Bay and Upernavik.

Naturally, stocks have been affected by these fisheries. Current stocks of Greenland Halibut only contain a small proportion of larger fish. Ten years ago half the fish caught at Ilulissat weighed more than 3.5 kilos. Nowadays only one out of every 10 fish caught is bigger than that.

During the last 10 years catches from *inshore waters* have increased from 7,000 tons (1987) to 19,000 tons (1996). In 2000, a total quota of 18,300 tons was recommended for the Disko Bay, Uummannaq and Upernavik area.

Greenland Halibut catches in *open sea areas* consist mainly of smaller fish – mostly immature females. Taking these fish before they have produced the next generation makes no sense whatsover, particularly when so little is known about the Greenland Halibut's reproduction cycle.

Since 1989, fishing for Greenland Halibut in East coast open sea areas has been at a stable, albeit high level, with 1,200 tons landed in 1996. Spawning stocks are estimated to be at a historically low level due to intensive fishing. This has sounded alarm bells for the Greenland Home Rule Government's scientific advisors, who are worried about increased Greenland Halibut catches, especially as critical information about the commercial fisheries is inadequate.

Fishing for Greenland Halibut using trawls and gill nets produces secondary catches – primarily Redfish and Grenadier, and quantities of smaller Halibut under the minimum size of 45 cm.

Trawl dredges, wires and nets damage the seabed, though long-term effects on seabed fauna are unknown. Compared to trawl and net fishing methods hook and line fishing results in far fewer secondary catches, but fishermen lose thousands of hooks and lines every year, and locals fear the knock-on effect. Sharks have been caught by fishermen in the Upernavik area with up to 200 old hooks in their stomachs.

Atlantic Cod *(Gadus morhua)* ↓

Experts from ICES and NAFO have recommended a total ban on Cod fishing in Greenland waters – whether open sea or sheltered. Additionally, ICES and NAFO have recommended that secondary catches of Cod associated with the shrimp fisheries be reduced.

The early 1970s saw the disappearance of the important West Greenland Bank Cod from fishing grounds. Furthermore, from the end of the 1980s no large quantities of Iceland Cod were observed migrating to the area. Today, the only Cod remaining are coastal Cod, which spawn in fiords.

From 1990 to 1992 Cod fisheries' catches fell from 130,000 tons to 17,104 tons, and from 1992 there was effectively no fishing of open sea Cod. Today, Fishing for Cod in sheltered waters is also economically insignificant. Catches declined from 5,700 tons in 1992 to a mere 700 tons in 1996.

Cod catches 1955–1997.

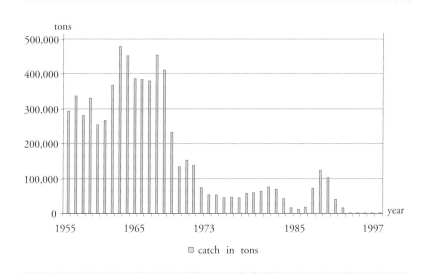

Source: *Technical report no 17, 1998, Greenland Institute of Natural Resources.*

Analyses of Cod populations show that stocks of open sea Bank Cod collapsed as early as the middle of the 1970s – most likely because of over fishing. Climatic changes to the sea around Greenland may subsequently have contributed to stocks never reviving. Declines in sheltered water stocks of Bank Cod can be attributed to heavy fishing combined with stocks failing to revive.

Pound net fishing for Cod rarely results in a large secondary catch, and undersize fish can escape alive out of the trap. Gill nets may produce small secondary catches of Sea Scorpions, Crabs and Greenland Halibut. However, many gill nets are lost on important fishing grounds and this can be a problem because these 'ghost' nets carry on fishing. In certain areas municipal authorities actually carry out clean-ups of lost fishing nets at important fishing locations.

Redfish *(Sebastes spp.)* ↓

NAFO recommends that there should be no fishing in waters off *West Greenland* until stocks have increased. Furthermore, NAFO has indicated that an effort be made to reduce the level of secondary catches of Redfish associated with shrimp fisheries.

With regard to *East Greenland*, ICES recommends that there should be no primary fishing for large Redfish, and that fishing for deep sea Redfish be further reduced by 25 per cent in all areas. ICES also recommends that Redfish catches on the continental shelf and in the Irminger Sea be reduced to a catch level not exceeding 85,000 tons.

Atlantic Salmon *(Salmo salar)* ↓

Atlantic Salmon are still found along Greenland's coastlines during the period August to November, when Salmon migrate in search of food from the American and European continents. Of these Salmon stocks 65 per cent originate from North America, with 35 per cent coming from Europe. There are very few Greenland Salmon as there is only one spawning river.

Originally, Salmon fishing was on a modest scale in sheltered waters. When the Salmon fishery was commercialised at the start of the 1960s, Danish, Norwegian and Faroese fishing vessels flooded into West Greenland to share in the Salmon bonanza.

Ten years later the party was over. The fishery peaked at the beginning of the 1970s with annual catches of over 2,500 tons. Since then catches have fallen to virtually nothing. Salmon fishing by foreign boats in Greenland waters was definitively halted in 1976. Twenty years later Greenland fishermen landed only 92 tons of Salmon. But even this catch – numbering some 33,750 fish – remains the subject of criticism, and was regarded as a threat to the survival of the species.

In 1997, ICES estimated that there were only about 197,000 large Salmon of North American origin left in the North Atlantic. Twenty years earlier estimated numbers were 850,000. The Salmon crisis has not only hit North America. In Ireland average Salmon catches have fallen from 600,000 fish less than twenty years ago to only 120,000 fish in 1997.

Following 1997, when Greenland had a Salmon quota of 57 tons, ICES made annual recommendations for a total cessation of Salmon fishing in the West Greenland areas. However, the organization was forced to allocate a local (aboriginal subsistence) quota of 20 tons. Simultaneously ICES wants to identify better methods for estimating annual private consumption catch sizes in West Greenland.

There is no doubt that stocks in the Atlantic Ocean have been heavily reduced over the past decades. Indeed many research circles regard salmo salar as being on the road to extinction. Despite a certain number of positive developments in recent years, all indications point to stocks being at unacceptably low levels. This also means that 'Salmon spawning countries', not least of all USA, are very aware of developments in countries like Greenland.

Arctic Char *(Salvelinus alpinus)* ↓

Found everywhere in Greenland, Arctic Chars are the most northerly of all fresh water fish. The fish do not migrate long distances at sea but remain close to river systems from where they originated. Some types of Arctic Char never leave fresh water habitats.

Nylon gill nets are used for catching migrating stocks, which form the prime fishery. By far the largest numbers of Char migrate back to waters where they originally hatched. For this reason there are countless local populations of Char with little inter-breeding with other stocks.

The Arctic Char is a slow-growing species and populations in individual rivers are small. For this reason, individual local stocks do not tolerate excessively heavy fishing. Arctic Chars have been over fished in many rivers over the course of time by local fishermen, who have completely blocked upstream access for spawning fish by placing gill nets across the rivers. In particular, the commercial trade in Arctic Char has been the reason why stocks in many rivers have totally collapsed.

The Arctic Char plays an important part in Greenland households, and traditional summer fishing trips are still appreciated by many families. On paper, regulations for this popular form of fishing are extremely detailed. There would be little cause for alarm about the future of this fish if laws were respected.

Information is non-existent on the numbers of Arctic Char caught annually, but Char fishing is certainly increasing in line with private dinghies numbers and the building of summer houses in fiords (see also p. 40).

Abandoned and unattended nets can result in birds drowning. Divers, Eiders and White-tailed Eagles have all been found drowned in abandoned nets – despite a ban on leaving fishing nets personally unattended. Discarded nets are also increasingly causing environmental problems.

Other species of fish

In 2001, NAFO recommended that there should be no primary fishing in waters around West Greenland for stocks of the following: Grenadier (*Coryphaenoides rupestris*), Long Rough Dab (*Hippoglossoi-*

des platessoides), Ray/Skate (*Hypotremata* sp.) and Spotted Wolffish (*Anarhichas minor*). Secondary catches resulting from shrimp fisheries should at the same time be reduced to the lowest possible levels.

Towards sustainable exploitation
What needs to be done?

'We can no longer wait for biological information on declining stocks to be 100 per cent reliable before adjusting hunting pressure. Indeed, as politicians we have to take the risk of implementing restrictions on the basis of evidence that populations are declining to ensure more optimal management of wildlife – in the same way as doctors are duty bound to act before *the patient expires.'*

Alfred Jakobsen, Minister of Health and Environment. Quoted in AG/Grønlandsposten newspaper on 20 March 2001.

Those times, where everybody could harvest Greenland's living resources unhampered, are long since passed. Not least of all if the rhetoric on sustainable exploitation is to be taken seriously.

Actually, there is a range of options available for implementing this rhetoric. Over the last ten years the Greenland Home Rule Government has quietly tested most of the recognised measures, but efforts have been less than half-hearted. Enforcement has been nil with correspondingly minimal results.

Over the same decade the Greenland Home Rule Government has actually taken considerable steps *back* in time:

• Efforts to reduce hunting pressure on Guillemots in 1988 were halted after 16 months. Legislators had voted that Guillemot hunting should be reserved for professional hunters, but the measure was allegedly stopped after Members of Parliament and Ministers discovered that they also had to give up leisure hunting.
• Permission in Illoqqortoormiut/Scoresbysund allowing purchases for export of Guillemots shot during 1988–1990 summer hunting.
• Acceptance by the Home Rule Government of the increased commercial trade in Belugas with the approval of a factory ship operated by NuKa A/S.

- Decision in 2000 by the Parliament to allow commercial egg collection.
- Resolution by the Home Rule Government to increase Crab and Scallop quotas despite warnings from biologists.

Critics of this inadequate management of living resources have tended to particularly target Greenlanders who have registered themselves as professional hunters, but this is an over-simplification of the situation.

The number of *professional hunters* has fallen sharply in recent years. According to the Ministry of Industry numbers have dropped by half during the last seven years from 4,068 in 1993 to 2,569 in 2000. By contrast, there has been a significant rise in *leisure hunters* from 5,455 in 1993 to 8,094 in 2000.

It is unclear what hidden factors are behind this shift. For example, how many people temporarily register themselves as professional hunters in order to grab a share of extremely generous subsidy schemes for buying dinghies, engines and hunting equipment? How many, including women and children, register themselves as leisure hunters merely to grab a share of the Caribou quotas? And how many Greenlanders go hunting and fishing without being registered at all?

The answers are simply not known, but if it is true that a genuine shift is occurring in the way professional and leisure hunters use resources, then it is important for this shift to be incorporated in legislation. The transformation from a hunting culture to a subsidy-dependent culture should also be taken into consideration. Annual sealskin purchases alone cost the Greenland Home Rule Government DKK 35 million.

Nowadays professional hunters are totally dependent on a whole range of social subsidies aimed at limiting the exodus from small settlements and reducing unemployment. By 1994 it was already established that professional hunters as a population group could only enjoy acceptable living standards by virtue of large subsidies. Hunting families themselves only earn about 1/15 of an average income, and profits in the professional hunting business are just about non-existent.

In the longer term there can be little doubt that, for modern Greenlanders, good hunting and angling opportunities will be increasingly important as *leisure activities.* The major challenge will be to ensure a reasonable yield for professional hunters – or provide alternative occupations – while at the same time allowing the increasing number of leisure hunters to thrive. Currently there is nothing to indicate that living resources are sufficient to support the current activities of both groups.

Workable measures

Modern wildlife management control measures either involve regulating harvest *access* to living resources, or introducing yield amount *limits.*

In plain terms: In the long run it is unworkable to allow everyone to shoot or catch unlimited numbers of everything. And restrictions, rules and bans written on official Home Rule Government notepaper in Nuuk/Godthåb are totally inadequate if these are not efficiently enforced and controlled out in the hunting areas.

The following suggestions summarise the measures that can contribute to sustainable exploitation:

Close seasons
At the very least there should be peace for all species during the breeding season so populations can produce the next generations. In most other countries hunting during breeding seasons is generally prohibited for ethical and animal welfare reasons. It would also be highly beneficial to species if close seasons could be extended to include the mating seasons in early spring. In addition these measure could be used to protect particular groups within populations, similar to those applying to female Polar Bears with cubs.

Conservation areas
Restrictions on landing at, and moving around in wildlife conservation areas will safeguard habitats and allow stocks to breed in peace.

Conservation areas can play a positive role in stimulating outdoor activities and eco-tourism. The problems connected with the lack of implementation of Ramsar locations all too clearly illustrate that wildlife conservation areas have no meaning if they only exist on paper (See Chapter 1, p. 26 ff.). The same applies to the situation of the 5 km zones prohibiting noise around bird cliffs. If wildlife conservation areas are to be effective then there has to be efficient information and control, otherwise the effect is nil.

Hunting methods and equipment

Tighter regulations on weapon types, methods of transport and, for example, net mesh sizes can all reduce exploitation. These restrictions already apply to catches of Belugas and Minke Whales and a wide range of fish species, but unless rules are enforced such measure alone cannot guarantee results. With regard to legal egg collection, this 'harvesting method' is extremely damaging for bird colonies because they are massively disturbed by repeated waves of egg collectors. Most countries have legislation prohibiting random egg collection.

Hunting permits

Implementation of a proper hunting test and corresponding rifle test would be a major step in the right direction. Different types of permits can be issued allowing limited wildlife resources to be reserved for specific professional groups – for example professional hunters or leisure hunters. Today, some high-profile species including Walruses, Polar Bears (which sheep farmers can also hunt), Minke and Fin Whales can only be exploited by people holding professional hunting permits. However, anyone can hunt Belugas, Narwhales and Caribou. The ways in which the system operates today fortunately discourage hunting tourism.

An attempt to limit hunting of Brünnich's Guillemots in 1988 by reserving them for professional hunters had to be abandoned after 16 months due to widespread popular opposition. These protests came not least from members of the Greenland Parliament when they discovered that their rights to go 'Guillemot' hunting would be curtailed.

Quotas

Can be applied to specific areas or stocks but can also be targeted at individuals by the use of permits. This practice already applies to shrimps, fish and whales. Permits can be socially difficult to manage, because of the high risk of favouritism. This is especially true of the highly sought after shrimp quotas which can turn a fisherman into a millionaire in a single fishing season.

The rule applying to Guillemots and Eiders is that leisure hunters can kill a maximum of 5 birds per hunting trip, while no limits apply to professional hunters. Caribou hunting is also subject to quotas, though in this case quotas are adjusted every year according to the size of individual stocks. Muskox hunting permits are sold, and these are also available to non-residents.

The quota allocation system for Caribou and Muskox is also age dependent. Leisure hunters must be at least 16 years old when applying for permits.

Limiting commercial sales

Kill numbers are considerably influenced by the existence of a commercial market. At the present time, tens of thousands of Brünnich's Guillemots are sold either at the 'brættet' market in Nuuk or to trading companies like NuKa A/S. Numbers killed would fall dramatically if this possibility were removed. Banning the sale of Guillemots was a key factor in the efforts of the Canadian government to bring Guillemot hunting around Newfoundland under control. There is no doubt that a considerable reduction in Beluga catches could be achieved, if export of *mattak* to southern Greenland was banned.

Suggestions for positive initiatives

Wildlife protection laws and numerous hunting and trapping regulations from the Home Rule Government have not prevented the decline of living resources. While most measures taken have undoubtedly been correct these have neither been forcefully nor efficiently implemented.

If threatened species are to be preserved for the future, immediate action needs to be taken now. A summary of proposals is listed below.

Birds

A general ban of springtime hunting for most species has been introduced under new legislation from 1 January 2002, but all species should be included.

Also all egg collection should be banned. There should be better control of illegal hunting and traffic to bird colonies, and stronger restrictions on commercial trading. As a general rule all bird species with no commercial value should be totally protected. More simple blanket restrictions applying to all species should be implemented – e.g. uniform hunting season opening and closing dates.

Brünnich's Guillemot	Total ban on summer hunting; hunting ban within 5 km radius of colonies; aircraft ban within 5 km of colonies; hunting-free areas at wintering sites; hunting to end everywhere at the latest on 31 January; greater restrictions on sale of birds.
Common Eider	Access ban to breeding colonies; access ban to important moulting sites; hunting-free areas at wintering sites; ban on shooting at flocks; hunting to end on 31 January; setting up of a network of protected breeding reserves; restrictions on sale of birds.
King Eider	Identical hunting season as Eider; access ban to important moulting sites; hunting-free areas at overwintering sites; ban on shooting at flocks; restrictions on sale of birds.
Arctic Tern	Access ban to breeding colonies.
Geese	Ban on spring hunting for all species.
Other bird species	As a general principle all bird species with no commercial or nutritional value should be totally protected.

Marine mammals

In general, quotas should be implemented for all species to provide wildlife management with the necessary mechanisms for controlling development. A total hunting ban during the breeding season, and on females with young, should form a natural part of any modern society's legislation. Making better use of meat from animals killed will also need to be closely examined. This applies especially to meat from the sizeable seal and Caribou kills and the huge amounts of meat from larger whales.

Polar Bear	Quotas and quota enforcement; increased research.
Walrus	Total hunting ban; increased research; access ban near all traditional haul-out sites.
Ringed Seal	No restrictions; need for better utilisation of sealskins and especially meat.
Harbour Seal	Total hunting ban; increased research; access ban near all traditional haul-out sites.
Bearded Seal	Ban on sealskin trade; increased research.
Harp Seal	No restrictions; need for better utilisation of sealskins and especially meat.
Hooded Seal	Increased research.
Beluga	Quotas (max. 100 per year); enforcement of regulations; restrictions on commercial trade; better use of whale meat.
Narwhal	Quotas; enforcement of regulations; restrictions on commercial trade; better use of whale meat.
Minke Whale	Quotas; increased research; control of illegal hunting; ban on use of rifles; considerable need for better use of whale meat.
Fin Whale	Quotas; increased research; control of illegal hunting; considerable need for better us of whale meat.

Terrestrial Mammals

Caribou	Quotas; better organisation of trade and production so as to limit the amount of wasted meat.
Muskox	Quotas; better organisation of trade and production so as to limit the amount of wasted meat.

Fish

The general view is that quotas need to be allocated, more in line with scientific advice. A complete Salmon fisheries ban would not only benefit stocks but also improve relations with the USA.

Greenland Halibut	Stricter quotas.
Cod	Stricter quotas.
Redfish	Stricter quotas.
Atlantic Salmon	Total fisheries ban.
Arctic Char	Stricter quotas; increased local conservation; greater control

Shrimps, Crabs and Bivalves

In general, if the opportunity for sustainable exploitation of stocks is to be preserved in future, there is considerable need for fixing smaller quota sizes as specified by biologists. There also appears to be an urgent need for technological development of less destructive catching equipment.

Deep Sea Shrimp	Quotas; reduction in the amount of discarded secondary catches.
Snow Crab	Quotas as specified by biologists; local conservation.
Scallop	Ban on catches/local conservation; development of less destructive catching equipment.

Enforcement required

No matter which measures are chosen, effective enforcement of hunting and fishing is paramount. This applies particularly to a society like Greenland where 'hunting rules only apply within sight of a township' (see p.24 'Hunting laws – what hunting laws?').

In addition there are problems due to lukewarm Police attitudes to breaches of wildlife and environment laws (see chapter 2 p. 57 ff.). This calls for a concerted effort to heighten Police awareness and accountability for enforcing these sections of Greenland law.

Up to the present time – and where more than one out of every five inhabitants goes hunting – the Home Rule Government has only authorised the deployment of hunting and fishing enforcement officers at eight locations in this enormous country. Each location has one officer and one assistant assigned to it. With no police powers these 16 individuals have to maintain control of a hunting area the size of England. Suspected breaches of hunting, trapping and fishing regulations have to be reported by the officers to the police. The whole operation is financed by the Ministry of Industry, which also assigns tasks to the officers.

A major step forward towards controlled sustainable exploitation would be the creation of a regular corps of wildlife officers or *rangers* similar to the American model. This corps should consist of energetic and well educated Greenlanders willing and able to take over the role as hunting officers, reservation wardens, hunting consultants, wildlife advisors, etc., and also conduct censuses and report on wildlife stocks. These *rangers* could also play a positive role in the development of wildlife tourism and would be ideal as guides for larger groups of tourists. It would be very important to train this corps in the use of local hunting knowledge so as to unify this information with modern wildlife management methods.

At least two such officers should be stationed in each of Greenland's 17 towns with 1 or 2 part-time employees in each of the 59 settlements. Preferably, these people should not be hired locally and job rotation at regular intervals should occur in all cases to safeguard staff autonomy and to minimise the risk of corruption. The *corps* should be under the jurisdiction of the Police. The organisation could be financed by levies on kills, and a hunting permit tax, or by reducing the sealskin-purchasing subsidy.

No overnight miracles

Above all, Greenland's politicians and intellectuals need to take the bull by the horns and make it clear to everyone in Greenland society that there are no miracle cures for restoring living resources in one or two years. More realistically this will take generations.

What *can* be achieved right now is to slow down or stop the continuing decline of many species so that the situation no longer deteriorates. This applies particularly to Brünnich's Guillemot, Common Eider, Arctic Tern, Beluga, Narwhal, Walrus and Harbour Seal. After that it will be an uphill struggle for many years to come.

As an example we can look at how long it will take for extinct Guillemot colonies to return – if that is at all possible. An estimated calculation by the Greenland Institute of Natural Resources revealed that it would take decades of total conservation before positive results were observed.

Short-term conservation is totally ineffectual. This was demonstrated when an attempt was made to save the famous Salleq bird cliff in the Uummannaq municipality. By 1969 it was already clear that Salleq's once huge Brünnich's Guillemot colony was under threat. Barely 10,000 birds were all that remained of a colony that originally hosted in excess of 100,000 birds on the steep cliff sides.

Between 1969–72 a municipal conservation order was placed on the Salleq colony but it had no effect. Aside from doubts as to whether this conservation order was respected, Guillemots continued to be shot while away from colonies. Additionally, Guillemots reproduce so slowly that even under the most optimal conditions – in other words total all-year-round protection of every bird – it would take a minimum of 12 years before stocks doubled. A more realistic scenario reveals that it will take at least 35 years before there are twice as many birds.

Even with a genuine spring hunting ban in place, resurgence in the decimated colonies south of Upernavik Isfjord will not be measurable for many years to come. On the other hand, fatal declines in stocks can happen all too rapidly.

Based on the experience of the now extinct Salleq colony in Uummannaq the Greenland Institute of Natural Resources produced an estimated calculation that illustrated how slowly Guillemot stocks would regenerate. It is worth noting that these calculations also show the enormous losses that affect hunters once a colony is exterminated:

- The population at Salleq previously numbered approx. 100,000 birds. From other surveys we know that this figure corresponds to 70,000 breeding pairs and this brings the total number of birds connected to the colony to about 173,000. In addition about 29,000 sexually immature juveniles from the colony stay at other locations. All in all about 202,000 birds had their original address at Salleq.
- On the basis of these figures it was assumed that the population could tolerate an annual 'harvest' of 350 birds for every 1,000 breeding pairs. This provided hunters in the Uummannaq district with opportunities to shoot approx. 10,780 birds annually (5,600 adult birds and 5,180 juveniles). In wintering areas, hunters would be able to take an even bigger bite of the cherry and shoot 13,720 juveniles hatched the previous summer.
- But Uummannaq hunters shot far more birds than this and eventually exterminated the colony. To put it bluntly, hunters simply 'harvested' all 202,000 birds. This corresponds to the numbers that might have been harvested during 16 years of 'sustainable exploitation' in the Uummannaq district.
- By the mid-1980s, 100 birds were all that remained of the once majestic Salleq colony. If these were left to breed, and not subjected to any hunting or egg collection whatsoever, stocks could grow at a rate of 2–5.9 per cent annually. Theoretically this means that – and depending on whether growth rates were 2 or 5.9 per cent – populations on these cliffs could recover to 100,000 birds (70,000 breeding pairs) somewhere between *120* and *350* years from now.
- If, from 1940 onwards, hunters from the Uummannaq district had

only carried out 'sustainable exploitation' of the Salleq colony for the entire period of 120 and 350 years respectively, then total yields during this time would have been between 1.3 and 3.8 million birds, with an additional 1.6–4.8 million Guillemots available for winter hunting further south. In all, total yields could have been 14 to 45 times greater than those achieved by exterminating the Salleq colony.

Eider farming

These calculation on the theoretical Guillemot harvest at Salleq are just brain-teasers, but respect for this logic and private ownership has allowed the Faroese to exploit their bird colonies for centuries.

There are also ongoing and convincing examples from Iceland of sustainable exploitation of bird colonies. Shooting Eider is prohibited in Iceland. However, there is a long tradition of Eider down collection. There are currently about 350 Eider colonies all over the country and these operate as regular 'Eider Farms', where nesting down is systematically collected from nests once birds have left them.

These farms are looked after by an equivalent number of people or families who can produce a total of nearly 3,000 kilos of duck down per year. With current prices around DKK 6,000 per kilo this production amounts to an annual market value of approx. DKK 18 million.

The total Eider population in Iceland is currently estimated to comprise 250,000–300,000 pairs, with about 70 per cent of the total nesting at Eider farms. On average 60–70 nests are capable of producing one kilo of Eider down.

Eider exploitation in Iceland is an illustrative example of sustainable exploitation or 'wise use', as populations are increasing simultaneously. Similar activities could probably be set up in Greenland if some of the traditional colonies were protected and given the chance to grow to a reasonable size. This will require the setting up of some sort of private ownership system for colonies.

Nature conservation the Danish way

The 1980 Nature Conservancy Act is the only legal instrument in Greenland, which wildlife management can use to preserve wildlife areas. The law is outdated and actually offers no possibilities for protecting wildlife in Greenland against the presence of real threats.

By and large, the Act has been inoperative (as set out in chapter 1, p. 22 ff.). Additionally, the few areas already protected have never been actively managed. This also applies to the 11 designated Ramsar sites, which were agreed by the Greenland Home Rule Government as early as 1987, none of which were implemented in legislation and thus have never been actively managed.

The Ministry of Environment and Nature pointed this out in a discussion paper for a wildlife protection workshop in 1999, stating that: *'The bulk of current preservation orders are mostly bureaucratic measures, which in reality do not protect wildlife against actual threats.'*

The Act is a copy of an old Danish Nature Conservancy Act, which enables specific areas to be safeguarded against overexploitation. Amongst other things, the Act includes protection of areas against disturbances, including traffic access, building construction, and other human activities. However, the Act is not specifically designed to protect areas against hunting – the only real threat to wildlife in Greenland.

A major overhaul of this antediluvian Act has been in the pipeline at the Ministry of Environment and Nature for a very long time, and as early as 1996 the Ministry announced that it was on the way. Amendments were supposed to be presented for public discussion in spring 2001, but nothing happened.

A year earlier in February 2000, the Greenland Institute of Natural Resources published a report entitled 'Wildlife protection in Greenland'. This comprehensive report is worth studying because it forms an important element of the technical basis for revising the inadequate 1980 Nature Conservancy Act.

Amongst other things, the report *proves* that the majority of sensitive habitats found in Greenland are seldom, or never found in the few protected areas. This applies to stands of Birch, numerous rare plant habitats, homeothermic springs, salt lakes, King Eider moulting sites, Scallop banks and Narwhal summer habitats. Furthermore, the report *assesses* that King Eider moulting sites and stands of Birch face acute threats.

The report *recommends* that the Greenland Home Rule Government should protect considerably more areas. This especially applies to southern Greenland sheep farming districts where natural vegetation not already devastated by sheep grazing needs to be maintained and areas protected from technological intervention. In a direct reference to the positive experiences from nature reserves in Denmark, the report also recommends hunting and disturbance-free areas be designated for Common and King Eiders at all important foraging locations, breeding sites, and wintering locations.

Stated plainly: Eiders should be allowed to breed, moult and eat in peace.

Only harvesting the interest and leaving the capital intact sounds like common sense, but in Greenland things are unfortunately not that simple! The Ministry of Environment and Nature addressed the question in 1999 in a workshop discussion paper entitled 'Sustainable attitudes':

'In the Department we experience a tendency for many of the old hunting traditions to linger on today. Anything alive that moves is shot, and many hunters believe that when animals disappear from one area it is not because of hunting but simply that animals have moved to other places. Nobody seems to take into consideration that there are no other places for animals to go because physical distance no longer offers any protection to living resources.'

Ramsar sites as the linch pin

With exception of the North and Northeast Greenland National Park and also partly the Melville Bay nature reserve – which according to the Ministry of Environment and Nature is generally not respected – the 1987 list of 11 Ramsar sites (see p. 126) provides a vivid example of the need to protect key wildlife locations.

The special feature of Ramsar sites in Greenland is that they do not include any agricultural land. Consequently, Ramsar sites are not exposed to agricultural influences, or farming threats posed by drainage, cultivation, fertilization, manure storage, crop spraying etc. All threats to wildlife derive almost uniquely from traffic access – and hunting.

Designated Ramsar sites are discussed one by one in a topical report published in spring 2001 by NERI (The National Environmental Research Institute, Denmark). Contents, status and threats are meticulously described and the report presents a subsequent list of a further 16 important wildlife locations that could be protected for the benefit of both the environment and wildlife – and also hunters and trappers in the long term. The list of designated Ramsar sites, including the proposed new sites, is appended.

There can be little doubt that a well-run network of controlled and monitored Ramsar sites could be a pivotal influence in the regeneration of many hunted stocks of wildlife that are disappearing from Greenland.

It might be worth while, although it will take daring and a completely unorthodox move to implement the principle of 'cross compliance', thereby smoothing the path for local management in these areas, with a view to possibly bringing the negative developments to a halt. The 'cross compliance' principle really means 'scratch my back and I'll scratch yours', and is rapidly making its entry onto the EU Agricultural policy scene.

In Greenland's special context, and depending on circumstances, payments of fixed social subsidies to hunters and trappers should cease. Instead, subsidies should be regulated according to progress – or non-progress – in local management of living resources. For instance, subsidies would decrease if illegal egg collection or summer hunting continued, whereas an increase in breeding Eiders would trigger a subsidy increase.

Ramsar sites in Greenland: Status of existing sites, and proposed new areas.

Site no.	Present threats	Risk of conflict	Requires regulation
1. Aqajarua & Sullorsuaq	hunting, bivalve fishing, helicopter traffic	↑↑↑	↑↑↑
2. Qinnquara Marraa & Kuussuaq	hunting, bivalve fishing, helicopter traffic	↑↑	↑↑↑
3. Kuannersuit Kuussuat	no serious threats	↑↑	↑↑
4. Kitsissunnguit	egg collection, hunting, helicopter traffic	↑↑↑	↑↑↑
5. Naternaq	helicopter traffic and other activities	↑↑	↑↑
6. Eqalummiut Nunaat – Nassuttuup Nunaa	helicopter-traffic and other activities	↑↑	↑↑
7. Ikkattoq	hunting	↑↑	↑↑
8. Kitsissut Avalliit	egg collection, hunting, helicopter traffic	↑↑	↑↑↑
9. Heden	helicopter traffic	↑↑	↑
10. Hochstetter Forland	helicopter-traffic	↑	↑
11. Kilen	helicopter-traffic	↑	↑
Possible new sites			
Germania Land	helicopter-traffic	↑	↑
Itsako	hunting, helicopter-traffic	↑↑	↑↑↑
Umiiarfik	hunting, helicopter-traffic	↑↑	↑↑↑
Qilangaarsuit	hunting, helicopter-traffic, outdoors life	↑↑↑	↑↑↑
Foulke Fjord	no present threats	↑	↑
Hakluyt Ø	no present threats	↑	↑↑
Saunders Ø	no present threats	↑	↑↑
Kap York-Kap Atholl	no present threats	↑	↑↑
Kap Schackleton og Kipakku	egg collection, hunting, helicopter traffic	↑↑	↑↑↑
Søndre Isortoq	egg collection, hunting, helicopter traffic	↑↑↑	↑↑↑
Evighedsfjorden	egg collection, hunting, helicopter traffic	↑↑↑	↑↑↑
Sermilinnguaq	egg collection, hunting, helicopter traffic	↑↑↑	↑↑↑
Nipisat Sund	hunting	↑↑↑	↑↑↑
Kap Brewster	egg collection, hunting	↑↑↑	↑↑↑
Østed Dal, Colorado Dal, Enhjørningens Dal, Pingel Dal	helicopter traffic	↑	↑
Storsletten, Wollaston Forland	helicopter traffic	↑	↑

↑↑↑ *high risk;* ↑↑ *medium risk;* ↑ *low risk;* Source: *The Greenland Ramsar sites. NERI (The National Environmental Research Institute, Denmark), Technical Report, no. 346, 2001.*

Writing on the wall
Time is running out for Greenland

'For a Danish biologist, who sadly sees wildlife sources being rapidly depleted in his own country, it is liberating to be confronted with Greenland's magnificent and timeless Arctic world. While wildlife death sentences are being pronounced all over the world, we can still encounter pristine and wonderfully fascinating nature on our planet in these Arctic surroundings, and in uninhabited and trackless tropical mountain areas. But fate is also knocking on the door of these virgin territories and insatiable human expansion is also threatening these beautiful and tranquil worlds. Greenland will hopefully realise that the writing is on the wall – before it is too late.'

Salomonsen, Finn: Birds of Greenland. Rhodos, Copenhagen 1967.

These days, Greenland's hunting culture has been replaced by a *subsidy culture* – exceeding even the most grotesque EU farming subsidies. Professional hunters, dinghy fishermen and sheep farmers annually receive millions in subsidies from the Greenland Home Rule Government, without any prospect of Greenland society making reasonable use of what these groups catch or produce.

Thousands of seal carcasses are dumped into the sea after skinning. Whale carcasses are abandoned on the ice after valuable *mattak* has been flensed off. Dead Muskoxen are burnt, frozen Guillemots are driven to the municipal rubbish dump, Walrus carcasses are allowed to rot, and tons of shrimp and Halibut are dumped for the benefit of ravens and gulls because of insufficient capacity at food processing plants.

The Caribou situation is a chapter of its own. NuKa A/S was not fully able to use the 2000 quota of 13,260 animals, and the company feared that it would be inundated with tons of unsaleable meat from the 2001 hunting season. NuKa A/S is responsible for managing the purchase and distribution of thousands of tons of meat from kills based on the 2001 quota of 24,300 Caribou – half an animal for every Greenlander.

Meat wastage from Greenland kills is enormous. Thousands of tons of meat from killed animals and birds are not used at all. At the same time the quantity of beef and pork imported from Denmark satisfies three quarters of the population's needs.

According to Greenland's Agricultural Council, despite being awash with meat, Greenland's red meat *self-sufficiency* percentage is just 24 per cent – i.e. 76 per cent of the population's meat and meat products' consumption is imported. In Iceland the comparable self-sufficiency level is close to 95 per cent, while the level in Norway is 70 per cent.

Professional and leisure hunters annually kill birds and mammals in quantities that could easily supply the whole of Greenland society with 100 per cent traditional foods – with enough left over to feed the 25,000 hungry sledge dogs. To make matters worse there has been no coordinated attempt to rationally organize the use of kills, and more and more Greenlanders prefer to eat imported foods. Hence the very high wastage of meat that is otherwise fit for human consumption.

Not least of all, in view of this wastage (see p. 138), it is hard to defend the hunting and shooting of animals and birds when these activities are contributing to the eradication of Greenland's wildlife.

The writing is clearly visible in capital letters on the wall.

Subsidy culture

Over the past 20 years a whole range of statutory financial aid packages have been introduced to support Greenland's fishermen, hunters and farmers. These subsidies are given in the form of interest-bearing loans, interest-free/repayment-free loans, and guarantees on loans made by finance companies. Additionally, millions of Danish kroner are spent in support of companies that are partly or wholly owned by the Greenland Home Rule Government.

If a Greenlander wants to acquire a vessel for *professional fishing or hunting purposes*, total public financing can be as much as 92.5 per cent of the purchase price. Interest-free/repayment-free loans (i.e. direct subsidies) can represent up to 37.5 per cent of the total purchase price – including the cost of fishing gear, insurance premiums for three months, delivery charges, etc.

Up to 90 per cent of the total cost can be financed by public funding for major improvements, such as replacement of machinery and the purchase of safety equipment for existing vessels. Interest-free/repayment-free loans can cover 30 per cent of these expenses.

Dinghy fishermen and hunters also milk the Home Rule treasury. Subsidies of up to 75 per cent of the cost of dinghy purchases can be granted – and this can be as much as 84 per cent for dinghies used in the Qaanaaq district or in East Greenland. The scheme also covers fishing equipment, three months worth of insurance premiums, and supplementary delivery charges.

If a Greenlander decides to take up *farming* then subsidies are available that match even the most favourable EU rules. Buying, buildings or expanding buildings for agricultural purposes is made easy with farmers themselves only needing to fund 10 per cent of the cost. The public sector finances the rest with 75 per cent in interest-free/repayment-free loans and 15 per cent in interest-bearing loans. Subsidies are also available under a different scheme for Greenland farmers to purchase or build their own homes.

Greenland farmers can build their own power plants – with down payments of just 10 per cent – and get the remaining 90 per cent financed with 60 per cent funded by interest-free/repayment-free loans, and 30 per cent in interest-bearing loans. 90 per cent of the cost of hiring employees or buying snow-scooters is covered by interest-bearing loans. Acquiring machines, equipment and similar articles is likewise 57 per cent covered by interest-bearing loans, with 33 per cent in interest-free/repayment-free loans. Interest-free/repayment-free loans finance 70 per cent of the cost of ground improvements. The cost of irrigation equipment, fencing and similar projects can be 60 per cent financed with interest-free/repayment-free loans, with the remaining 30 per cent covered by interest-bearing loans.

Last but not least, purchases of animal feed and seed are financed by the public purse with interest-free/repayment-free loans for up to 100 per cent of the purchase price.

And even when a business hits the rocks, it is still possible to apply for interest subsidies to help reduce outstanding interest owed to private or public sector finance companies.

400 million kroner in sealskin subsidies

Subsidies are also available for the killing process. If a Greenlander wants to kill large whales he has to use harpoon grenades – and these are not cheap. But help is at hand and the Home Rule treasury steps in with a subsidy of DKK 3,400 for every grenade purchased. This covers about half the price.

However, the subsidy culture's most grotesque example is the way sealskin subsidies have been allowed to develop. It all began relatively modestly in 1981 when subsidies of DKK 7.8 million were paid out to hunters. At that time hunters were allegedly hard-hit by the international sealing boycott campaign – particularly around Newfoundland. By 2000 this cash-support pond had grown to a massive-subsidy lake worth DKK 37.4 million, in which even leisure hunters get to swim.

As shown by the figures below these subsidies have got out of hand with more than DKK 400 million paid out to hunters in just twenty years. This means that over the period in question the Greenland Home Rule Government has paid thousands of kroner in subsidies for every single Greenland fur coat worn by fashion-conscious European women.

Purchases of skins in Greenland, 1981–2001.

Year	Skins bought	Subsidy in DKK mil.	Subsidy per skin in DKK
1981	55,663	7.8	140
1982	55,211	9.2	167
1983	47,842	8.6	180
1984	52,514	9.6	183
1985	50,526	10.9	216
1986	data n/a	?	?
1987	data n/a	?	?
1988	57,545	13.9	241
1989	45,038	11.6	257
1990	53,471	15.1	282
1991	64,530	19.9	308
1992	69,140	20.4	295
1993	52,056	14.3	275
1994	60,339	19.8	328
1995	53,211	22.4	421
1996	76,267	30.6	401
1997	73,971	34.7	469
1998	83,752	36.3	433
1999	106,100	36.3 (44.4)	342 (419)
2000	102,700	37.4	364
2001	–	35.0	–

NB: The subsidies listed above are fixed under Greenland finance law, but extra subsidies may well have been paid in specific years by way of supplementary grants (e.g. DKK 8.1 million in 1999). Supplementary grants were abolished after 2000. Source: *staff info., Grønlands Skindindhandling (Greenland Fur Traders), 2001.*

Rotting skins and scandals

Although seal kills, and especially Harp Seals kills, have risen dramatically over the past 5 years, the quality of purchased skins has fallen noticeably.

The explanation, according to Grønlands Skindindhandling (Greenland Fur Traders), which purchases sealskins for the parent company

Great Greenland A/S, is that women no longer help with the curing process. Men it seems are not capable of doing women's work of drying and curing skins. This is the reason why purchasing has been switched to fresh and salted skins instead of dried skins. Undoubtedly this method results in reduced quality and far greater wastage.

Simultaneously, there have been noticeable differences in sealskin quality valuations between local areas and Grønlands Skindindhandling in Qaqortoq/Julianehåb. Between 1994–1999 there was a large increase in the number of grade 1 sealskins from local areas (i.e. skins fetching top prices). These valuations were not matched by the actual quality of the sealskins received at Greenland Fur Traders processing facility.

In 1999 for example, local buyers classified 69.4 per cent of all skins at grade 1 prices. Only 11.4 per cent were rated at grade 3. On delivery to Greenland Fur Traders only 33.3 per cent of skins conformed to grade 1 standards. Grade 3 skins accounted for 34 per cent. Not surprisingly Greenland Fur Traders had to pay the high valuation prices.

Record sealskin purchases in 1999 were characterised by the fact that many skins were simply rotten. Of the 105,741 sealskins purchased, 19,756 had to be destroyed. Nearly one in five skins (18.7 per cent) were thrown out – at a loss of DKK 9 million.

The problem with purchases of rotting skins has always existed, but has increased over the years. Additionally, warehouses are glutted with gradually deteriorating skins. Greenland Fur Traders is under an obligation to buy all sealskins brought in by hunters – irrespective of demand or sales potential. In times of falling demand, the stockpile of slowly deteriorating skins mushrooms. Sealskins preserved in brine for 10–15 years are often unusable when the time comes to turn them into furs.

As of 1 January 2000, 28,000 unsaleable sealskins lay stockpiled at Qaqortoq/Julianehåb. According to Greenland Fur Traders stocks are currently bulging with 70,000–90,000 raw skins.

The doubling in numbers of sealskins purchased between 1995–2000 corresponds to the rise in seal kills during the same period. Increased killing has resulted in an enormous wastage of meat –

wastage that in the long term can threaten the marketing of Harp Seal furs as exclusive 'sustainable' products. Nevertheless every year, hunters continue to dump thousands of skinned carcasses into the sea – no one can find a use for such large quantities of seal meat.

The newspaper Sermitsiaq has written about this wastage in several articles over the years. The latest appeared in March 2001:

'In the long term this enormous waste of resources will damage the romantic notion that Greenlanders kill hunted animals at a sustainable level. Without doubt, these condemned carcasses can damage the millions earned by Great Greenland's export of sealskins.(…) Expensive furs from Great Greenland are bought by sophisticated European women under the illusion that hunters use the entire seal. The real picture is completely different.(…)'

The image of wasted seal meat portrayed by the newspaper is worlds apart from the glossy advertising jargon used by Great Greenland in its marketing of Greenland sealskin products. Read more in chapter 2, p. 52 ff.

In 1999, an attempt to organize the seal meat trade developed into a full-blown scandal, and cost the Greenland taxpayer about DKK 50 million – without a single kilo of seal meat ever being sold! The intention was for the state owned company Puisi A/S to sell seal blubber at the unbelievable price of DKK 500 per kilo to a subsidiary company in China, which would manufacture health tablets and seal sausages for sale on the Chinese market. Greenland's Home Rule Government invested in machinery and production facilities prior to reaching any form for sales agreement on the Chinese market. The entire project was based on verbal agreements with an American businessman who guaranteed the Chinese part of the project. When a Greenland delegation visited China in December 1999 to inspect the Chinese factory they found the facility was non-existent. The American businessman disappeared without a trace. Puisi A/S was declared bankrupt a few months later.

The Home Rule Government has nevertheless attempted to control the subsidy culture. Additional grants for sealskin purchase were abolished in 2000, and several other fishing industry subsidies, including subsidised fuel, were removed – but not completely, as it turned out.

KNAPK, the fisherman's trade union that has political support from many Members of Parliament, had no intention of surrendering subsidies without a fight. This was illustrated in April 2001 when the Parliamentary Fisheries and Hunting Committee demanded implementation of *'a general minimum price for fish landed in Greenland'*. The chairman of the committee, Member of Parliament Johan Lund Olsen, said that *'the recent episodes, including the breakdown in negotiations on Greenland Halibut prices between Royal Greenland and KNAPK proved the necessity of fixing minimum prices for landed fish.'*

KNAPK supported the Committee proposal of minimum prices and fisherman took action on 1 May. They announced that if subsidies for shrimp and Greenland Halibut were not guaranteed they would blockade many of Greenland's harbours two days later. The Home Rule Government initially refused to comply with KNAPK's demands, but when fishermen blockaded several ports they got their way. The Home Rule Government was forced to back down and promise fishermen higher prices and millions in subsidies for shrimp and Greenland Halibut.

A few weeks later Greenland's Parliament reneged on its promise, and instead re-introduced a subsidised fuel package. Diesel subsidies totalling DKK 8 million were approved bringing the price down to DKK 1.53 per litre. Petrol was also subsidised to the tune of DKK 3.4 million with prices falling to DKK 2.85 per litre.

The big meat party

In March of 2001 Simon Olsen, Minister of Industry, commented on the large-scale wastage of seal meat referred to in an article published in the Sermitsiaq newspaper entitled 'Discarded seal carcasses – the sealskin time bomb'.

Simon Olsen warned: *'We have every reason to be concerned about attitudes from abroad, which can damage the hunting profession.'*

There is no doubt that the Minister's concern is well founded – especially as conservative estimates of annual hunting kills in Greenland reveal that huge quantities of living resources are wasted. Thousands of tons of meat are simply allowed to rot away every year.

It is relatively easy to produce a meat account for Greenland. Absolute minimum figures for annual animal and bird kills can be calculated with the help of kill statistics from *Piniarneq 2001*. The author has selected 1998, as this is the latest year for which statistics are available. Statistics on animal-weight averages are readily available from scientific literature as well as the average consumption of traditional food products. Thereafter it is a question of simple mathematics. In 1998 Greenland's indigenous population numbered 50,000 people. The total population including other nationalities, most of them Danish, was 58,000.

The resulting calculation demonstrates (see the table of figures below) that:

at least 17,500 tons of animals and birds are killed annually – corresponding to 350 kilos of meat per indigenous Greenlander.

Based on numerous research reports it is possible to conclude that at least 40 per cent of this gross meat weight is fit for human consumption. This means that there is *a minimum* of 7,000 tons of meat available for consumption by the population – or 140 kilos for every Greenlandic man, woman and child. For Greenlanders this amounts to an average daily ration of 384 grams of meat from hunted animals – 365 days a year.

But according to studies by *Kapel & Petersen 1982* and *Pars 2000,* the daily requirement of meat is only 315 grams (plus approx. 90 grams of fish).

This means that even if bird and mammal kills were the Greenland population's only sources of poultry and meat there would be an annual surplus of 1,250 tons – or 25 kilos of meat for every Greenlander.

Greenland meat account for 1998.

Species	Kills 1998 (Piniarneq 2001)	Weight per kill in kilos	Total weight in tons	Weight per Greenlander in kilos
Brünnich's Guillemot	221,783	0.9	200	4.0
Common Eider	72,109	1.5	108	2.1
King Eider	3,362	1.5	5	0.1
Black Guillemot	30,517	0.375	11	0.2
Little Auk	21,017	0.15	3	0.06
Black-legged Kittiwake	43,713	0.4	17	0.34
Rock Ptarmigan	45,156	0.4	18	0.36
Harbour Porpoise	2,131	70	149	3.0
Pilot Whale	365	2,500	912	18.2
Beluga	746	900	671	13.4
Narwhal	822	1,200	986	19.7
Minke Whale	187*	7,500	1,403	28.0
Fin Whale	9*	50,000	450	9.0
Polar Bear	198	500	99	2.0
Walrus	610	600	366	7.3
Muskox**	592	200	118	2.4
Caribou***	3,692	110	406	8.1
Polar Hare	3,707	3.9	15	0.3
Ringed Seal	82,108	50	4,105	82.1
Harp Seal	82,491	70	5,774	115.5
Hooded Seal	6,328	200	1,266	25.3
Bearded Seal	2,354	200	471	9.4
Total			17,553	350.8

* Quota for year (1998), ** 2001 quota was 1,200, *** the quota for 2000 was fixed at 13,260 animals with recommended quota of 24,300 animals for 2001 – corresponding to a kill weight of 2,763 tons or 46 kilos of Caribou per inhabitant if the entire quota were killed.

Greenland's production of lamb is not included in the above table. According to NuKa A/S stockpiles of lamb amount to about 250 tons annually. This corresponds to 4.3 kilos of lamb per inhabitant.

According to Statistics Greenland, and in spite of the copious quantities of meat made available from hunting, Greenland annually imports about 3,400 tons of meat and meat products. If lamb and imported meat were included in the meat account calculations for the whole population, the annual meat surplus would grow considerably. As most meat imports are likely to be consumed immediately, it is fair to assume that meat surpluses would invariably come from hunted animals. A theoretical calculation (see table below) such as this points to the fact that:

approx. 4,000 tons of birds and mammals (57 per cent of total hunting kills) are never used for human consumption.

Use of hunting kills, Greenland production, and imported meat products in 1998.

Category	Total weight in tons
Mammals and birds killed in 1998	17,500
Meat suitable for consumption (40 per cent of kill weights)	7,000
Greenland sheep and lamb (slaughtered weight)	250
Imported meat products (ref. Statistics Greenland)	3,400
Total meat quantities available for consumption	**10,650**
Nutritional needs (0.315 kg x 58,000 inhabitants x 365 days)	6,669
Surplus of meat fit for human consumption	**3,981**
Hides, offal, etc (for dog food)	10,500
Import of cat and dog food (ref. Statistics Greenland)	365
Food needs for 25,000 sledge dogs (400 kg/year)	10,000
Surplus of meat bi-products for dog food	**865**

Sledge dogs eat dried dog food

Of course, kills have to cover some of the food requirements of Greenlands sledge dogs. These dogs eat just about anything. Traditionally they were fed on meat, blubber, offal from hunted animals, and fish and fish scraps. In a 1982 study, *Kapel & Petersen* calculated that Greenlands working sledge dogs needed to eat about 400 kilos of food annually. Other researchers, including *Born* (1987), have significantly downgraded this quantity to an annual intake of about 250 kilos.

As of 31 December 2000 the total sledge dog population in Greenland was 25,099. Numbers seem to be falling and all indications point to the fact that the use of sledge dogs for fishing and hunting purposes is declining rapidly. Sledges are increasingly being replaced by snow-scooters and nowadays dogs are mostly used for tourist trips, sledging competitions, and leisure hunting and fishing trips.

Sledge dogs' food requirements are calculated at somewhere between 6,250 and 10,000 tons annually. This is more than covered by the 60 per cent – at least 10,500 tons – of hunting 'leftovers' (blubber, offal, meat scraps etc.). Additionally there is nearly 4,000 tons of highly edible surplus meat from hunting, plus large quantities of fish and fish scraps, which is used as an important source of dog food in many places.

Some dogs however are not fed with meat from Greenland. Instead they are fed on imported dog food.

Statistics from as far back as 1982–83 showed that KGH imported about 40 tons of KING dried dog food to Illoqqortoormiut/Scoresbysund – home at that time to 1,000 sledge dogs. Figures from Statistics Denmark in 1998 revealed that Greenland imported 365 tons of packaged cat and dog food for retail sale to a value of DKK 3 million.

Too expensive to eat Greenland's own food

Meat wastage is put further into perspective when, as illustrated in the previous table, the considerable meat imports, particularly from Denmark, are included. According to Statistics Greenland about 3,400 tons of beef, pork, lamb, poultry, meat and meat products are imported into Greenland. This is equivalent to 59 kilos per inhabitant or 162 grams of meat products per day.

In reality, half the annual meat consumption is met by imports. Statistics Greenland reveals that annual imports of 'meat and other meat products' cost nearly DKK 100 million.

According to a University of Copenhagen PhD thesis in 2000, the consumption of traditional Greenland food products (seal meat, fish, whale meat and birds) represents no more than 22 per cent of the energy requirement in an average diet, and the figure is in sharp decline. In 1974, 89 per cent of Greenlanders ate traditional food products several times a week. By 1993–94 the figure had fallen to a mere 17 per cent. Out in the settlements inhabitants derive one third of their energy needs from traditional foods, but town dwellers only satisfy one fifth of their energy needs with traditional products.

The thesis contends that the principal factors for this fall in traditional food consumption are:

- Traditional foods are hard to come by.
- Products are too expensive.
- Consumers want a more varied diet.

Increasing discrepancies between large quantities of kills and poor utilisation have occurred – for three reasons: *the subsidy culture, prices,* and *changing eating habits.*

Extensive subsidies to professional hunters and sheep farmers contribute to maintaining hunting activities on a massive scale, with sales of animals and birds playing a lesser role. Guaranteed minimum prices and guarantees from Home Rule Government owned companies also contribute to this large-scale wastage.

At the February 2001 annual general meeting of Royal Greenland A/S, Chairman of the Board Uffe Ellemann-Jensen, explained the company's poor financial result with these words:

'We have purchased larger quantities locally than we could properly process and produce, and this has resulted in stock degradation, lower quality, and correspondingly lower prices.'

Royal Greenland A/S is Greenland's largest company. The annual turnover in 2000 was DKK 3.5 billion. Profits for that year were a mere DKK 11 million.

The other major problem is the high price of hunting products.

Imported foods have long since priced traditional food products out of the market.

In an April 2001 Sermitsiaq newspaper article, Keld Askær, CEO of the KNI supermarket chain stated:

'It is true that profit margins on imported meat are considerably higher than those applying to Greenland meat products. Not because profit margins on imported meat are excessive but because profits on traditional Greenland meat products are too low. We would very much like to sell more Greenland products but they are simply too expensive.'

Advertisements from Danish owned Brugsen supermarkets and other Nuuk/Godthåb chain stores highlight the considerable price difference between Greenland's traditional food products and imported meat products. A difference so great, that only few Greenland families could afford to live exclusively on traditional foods, if they had to buy them.

The table below shows a selection of prices from April 2001. Please note that Danish Moms (Value Added Tax) does not apply in Greenland.

Kilo prices for meat products in Nuuk/Godthåb, April 2001.

Product	Price per kilo in DKK
Daloon spring rolls (pack of 10)	22.15
Minced beef 2 kg.	29.95
Brünnich's Guillemot*	**30.00**
Seal meat*	**30.00**
Fresh chicken (thawed)	33.30
Minced pork (pack of 3)	33.35
Pork loin with rind	37.00
Minced beef	39.90
Eider*	**40.00**
Osso Buco	43.90
Sliced pork loin	44.95
Rolled joint of pork	49.90
Pork rib roast	49.90

Diced pork	49.90
Traditional roast beef	51.90
Tulip bacon	55.55
Rump steak	59.90
Sirloin steak	59.90
Cuvette	59.90
Minke Whale (diced)	**63.00**
Calf tongue	69.90
Smoked pork saddle	69.90
Pork chops	69.95
Greenland lamb (½ lamb, special offer)	**73.90**
Mutton for soup	**74.90**
Pork minion	79.35
Shrimps (2.5 kg pack)	**79.60**
Caribou (fresh)*	**80.00**
Pork steaks	83.35
Ammasatter (Capelin)	**93.90**
Wienersnitzel	109.90
Muskox	**115.00**
Saddle of lamb	**119.90**
Leg of lamb	**139.50**
Lamb chops	**151.50**
Entrecôte of beef	159.90
Greenland Smoked Halibut	**159.90**
Smoked Salmon	**159.90**
Beluga mattak	**160.00**
Uvak (winter dried cod)	**325.00**
Dried fish (Greenland speciality)	**350.00**
Wolffish (dried strips)	**350.00**

*Prices at the 'brættet' market in Nuuk/Godthåb. Source: *Nuuk Ugeavis, Brugsen Advertisements, visits to stores.*

Even with extra costs of long distance transport it is obvious that imported meat is far cheaper than Greenland products. Because Greenland is not in the EU export subsidies to Danish pork producers mean that meat imports have a competitive advantage over traditional products. However, subsidies are relatively modest and do not fully explain the large price differences. The EU paid subsidies of

DKK 9.3 million on Danish pork products exported to Greenland during the whole period 1995–2000.

No other obvious explanations immediately spring to mind as to why traditional Greenland products are so expensive, other than that professional hunters refuse to operate on market terms. Apparently, hunters prefer to allow huge quantities of meat to go to waste, instead of pricing their products competitively.

Another explanation is that traditional products such as seal meat are only sold at the 'brættet' market as large bloody chunks of meat and blubber. It is far easier, and much more appealing, for a modern Greenlandic housewife to go shopping in well-stocked supermarkets – and cheaper into the bargain! There can be no doubt that product development should be a high priority if all these considerable quantities of meat from hunting kills are to be used as food for human consumption.

Battle lines

More and more people in Greenland sense that developments are on the wrong track. Debates on subsidy cultures and the exploitation of declining resources have increased in recent years. These days the tone in Greenland's media can be as sharp as a flensing knife.

But what good are they? Will Greenland's leaders take the necessary initiatives before it is too late? Or will the overexploitation continue until the last Brünnich's Guillemot at Kingittoq is shot, and the last Beluga is dumped on the ice – *mattak* stripped?

Clearly the writing is on the wall. The gravity of how much is at stake is underlined by the many warnings provided by innumerable surveys and scientific reports. But will these reports be read?

The leader writer of the AG/Grønlandsposten newspaper has covered the overexploitation of Greenland's wildlife for more than 30 years. He has repeatedly warned against the ignorance, and the consequences of the careless way in which Greenlanders treat their wildlife resources and the environment. He has unambiguously and bravely stated what others – in a society where prevalent politically correct attitudes applaud the picture postcard image of the past – only dare to whisper.

His words, written in a leading article on 15 March 2001, are a fitting conclusion to this book.

' Self-opinionated hunters

We need to change our tune immediately, otherwise world consumer confidence in Greenland as a clean country with an exemplary approach to wildlife and environmental preservation will be eroded. In fact, as Denmark and Greenland's trading partners become aware of the real way in which we treat our wildlife, confidence in Greenland is starting to crumble.

Seafood exports from Greenland have been on a roll – helped by glossy sales brochures of pristine, snowy-white icebergs, clear-blue fiords and sunshine-filled skies. That is how we market our country. That is how the world sees Greenland. That is up to now!

But our reputation is tarnishing. Danish, and foreign newspapers and magazines are starting to write about the careless way Greenland treats its wildlife and environment. Conceited and supercilious attitudes result in policies of delay on wildlife and environment conservation.

The Greenland Institute of Natural Resources has published a white paper on Belugas – a well-researched report specifically aimed at hunters, which clearly explains the seriousness of the Beluga situation.

But hunters are not interested in listening to experts and professional advice from people in Greenland or from other countries. They consider their own observations carry far greater weight than all the world's research surveys, and brazenly value their haphazard (read: unsystematic) experiences as the only absolute truths.

But of course hunters are also interested in wildlife conservation. No hunter in this country wants hunting animals to disappear. If animals disappear hunters are extinct. The problem is therefore not disagreement about the end result but about the data on wildlife and hunting animals.

Hunters' fossilized self-serving and at times fanatical ('we are the only people who know') arguments preclude objective and honest discussions,

145

and blur the realities of the situation. Hunters' intransigent attitudes frighten off weak politicians, who think more about votes than about Belugas. Hunters have a strong hold on voting opinion. Somewhere or other we all have a hunter in our family, or at least we had one not so very long ago.

Those hunters who man the barricades, and make out they are smarter than the rest of us, fail to understand the situation and take a completely unreasonable defensive position. They would rather turn black to white and white to black than allow others to make decisions.

And they get their way. Politicians are simply afraid of following the advice given to them and instead have approved a quota that may lead to the disappearance of the Beluga over the next 50 years.'

Bibliography

Anon.: Virksomhedsberetning for Politiet i Grønland 2000. Nuuk 2001. 150 pages.

Anon.: Oversigt over beskyttelsesforanstaltninger, der har en konkret arealmæssig udbredelse. Oplæg til workshop, 26.-28. Oktober 1999. Direktoratet for Miljø og Natur, Grønlands Hjemmestyre, 1999.

Anon.: Válisti 2 – Fuglar. Náttúrufrædistofnun Íslands, Reykjavik 2000.

Anon.: Piniarneq 2000. Direktoratet for Erhverv, Grønlands Hjemmestyre, 1999.

Anon.: Piniarneq 2001. Direktoratet for Erhverv, Grønlands Hjemmestyre, 2000.

Anthon, H.: Pattedyr, krybdyr og padder. Politikens Forlag, 1985. 256 pages.

Boertmann, D.: An annotated checklist to the birds of Greenland. Meddr Grønland, Biosci. 38, 1994. 63 pages.

Boertmann, D. & C. Glahder: Grønlandske gåsebestande – en oversigt. DMU, faglig rapport nr. 276, 1999. 59 pages.

Boertmann, D., A. Mosbech, K. Falk & K. Kampp: Seabird colonies in western Greenland, (60°-79°30'N.lat.). NERI Technical Report No. 170, 1996. 150 pages.

Born, E.W.: Havpattedyr og havfugle i Scoresby Sund: fangst og forekomst. Rapport til Råstofforvaltningen for Grønland og Grønlands Fiskeri- og Miljøundersøgelser, 1983. (dupl.)

Born, E.W.: Aspects of present-day maritime subsistence hunting in the Thule area, northwest Greenland. In: Hacquebord, L. & Vaughan, R.: Between Greenland and America. Cross-cultural contacts and the environment in the Baffin Bay area. Arctic Centre. University of Groningen, The Netherlands 1987. 151 pages.

Born, E.W., Heide-Jørgensen M.P. & Davis, R.A.: The Atlantic walrus *(Odobenus rosmarus rosmarus)* in West Greenland. Meddr Grønland, Biosci. 40: 3–33, 1994.

Born, E.W., Gjertz I. & Reeves R.R.: Population assessment of Atlantic Walrus. Meddelelser nr. 138, Norsk Polarinstitut, 1995.

Born, E.W.(ed.): Grønlandske fugle, havpattedyr og landpattedyr – en status over vigtige ressourcer, 1. Oktober 1998. Teknisk rapport nr. 16. Grønlands Naturinstitut, 1998.

Born, E.W. & T.B. Berg: A photographic survey of walruses (Odobenus rosmarus) at the Sandøen haul-out (Young Sund, eastern Greenland) in 1998. Teknisk rapport nr. 26. Grønlands Naturinstitut, 1999.

Bure, K. (red.): GRØNLAND. Turistforeningen for Danmark. Årbog 1952–53. Ringkjøbing, 1952.

Burmeister, A.D.: Bestandsstatus af krabber (Chionoecetes opilio) ved Vestgrønland og biologisk rådgivning for 2000. Teknisk rapport nr. 22. Grønlands Naturinstitut, 2000.

Burnham, K.K.: One Hundred Year Bird Survey in Greenland Produces Shocking Results. The Peregrine Fund, Newsletter no. 31, 2000.

Due, R. & T. Ingerslev: Naturbeskyttelse i Grønland. Teknisk rapport nr. 29. Grønlands Naturinstitut, 2000.

Egevang, C. & Boertmann, D. 2001: The Greenland Ramsar sites, a status report. – DMU Technical Report no. 346, 96 pages.

Engelstoft, J.J.: Omplantning af kammuslinger, Clamys islandica, ved Nuuk. Teknisk rapport nr. 30. Grønlands Naturinstitut, 2000.

Falk, K. & K. Kampp: A manual for monitoring Thick-billed Murre Populations in Greenland. Teknisk rapport nr. 7. Grønlands Naturinstitut, 1997.

Falk, K. & K. Kampp: Monitering af lomviebestanden på Hakluyt Ø, Avanersuaq 1987–1997. Teknisk rapport nr. 15. Grønlands Naturinstitut, 1998.

Falk, K. & K. Kampp: Langsigtet moniteringsplan for lomvier i Grønland. Teknisk rapport nr. 18. Grønlands Naturinstitut, 1998.

Falk, K. & K. Kampp: Lomvien i Grønland: mulige effekter af forskellige bestandspåvirkende faktorer, og praktiske grænser for ressourceudnyttelse. Teknisk rapport nr. 38. Grønlands Naturinstitut, 2001.

Falk, K., K. Kampp & A.S. Frich: Polarlomvien i Østgrønland, 1995. Teknisk rapport nr. 8. Grønlands Naturinstitut, 1998.

Falk, K., K. Kampp & F.R. Merkel: Monitering af lomviekolonierne i Sydgrønland, 1999. Teknisk rapport nr. 32. Grønlands Naturinstitut, 2000.

Freese, C.H.: The Consumptive Use of Wild Species in the Arctic: Challenges and Opportunities for Ecological Sustainability. WWF Canada & WWF International Arctic Programme, 2000. 145 pages.

Frich, A.S.: Fuglelivet og dets udnyttelse på Grønne Ejland i Vestgrønland, juni 1996. Teknisk rapport nr. 1. Grønlands Naturinstitut, 1997.

Frich, A.S.: Lomviefangst i Grønland. Teknisk rapport nr. 2. Grønlands Naturinstitut, 1997.

Frich, A.S.: Kommerciel lomviefangst i Grønland 1990–96. Teknisk rapport nr. 3. Grønlands Naturinstitut, 1997.

Frich, A.S.: Lomviefangst i Nuuk vinteren 1995/96. Teknisk rapport nr. 4. Grønlands Naturinstitut, 1997.

Frich, A.S. & K. Falk: Jagtindsats og ederfuglefangst ved Nuuk. Teknisk rapport nr. 5. Grønlands Naturinstitut, 1997.

Frich, A.S.: Ederfuglefangst i Grønland 1993. Teknisk rapport nr. 9. Grønlands Naturinstitut, 1998.

Génsbøl, B.: Naturguide til Grønland. Gads Forlag 1999, 448 pages.

Heide-Jørgensen, M.P., M. Acquarone & F.R. Merkel: Flytællinger af fugle og havpattedyr i Vestgrønland 1998. Teknisk rapport nr. 24. Grønlands Naturinstitut, 1999.

Holm Jakobsen, B. et al.(ed.): Topografisk Atlas Grønland. Udgivet af Det Kongelige Danske Geografiske Selskab og Kort- og Matrikelstyrelsen. C.A. Reitzels Forlag, København 2000.

Jensen, D.B.(ed.): Grønlands Biodiversitet – et landestudie. Teknisk rapport nr. 27. Grønlands Naturinstitut, 1999.

Johansen, P., Asmund, G. & Riget, F. (1999): Blykontaminering af grønlandske fugle – en undersøgelse af polarlomvie til belysning af human eksponering med bly som følge af anvendelse af blyhagl. Danmarks Miljøundersøgelser. 27 pages. – Faglig rapport fra DMU nr. 299.

Kampp, K. & K. Falk: The birds of Ydre Kitsissut (Kitsissut Avalliit), Southwest Greenland. Meddr Grønland, Biosci.42, 1994. 25 pages.

Kampp, K., D.N. Nettleship & P.G.H. Evans: Thick-billed Murres of Greenland: status and prospects. BirdLife Conservation Series, no. 1: 133–154, 1994.

Kapel, F.O. & R. Petersen: Subsistence Hunting – the Greenland Case. Rep. Int. Whal. Commn (special issue 4), 1982.

Kinze, C.C.: Havpattedyr i Nordatlanten. Gads Forlag 2001. 191 pages.

Kristoffersen, F.: Jæger og Fangstmand. En bog om Vildtet og Jagten i Grønland. Nyt Nordisk Forlag-Arnold Busck. København 1969, 185 pages.

Lisborg, T.D. & J. Teilmann: Spættet sæl i Kangerlussuaq/Søndre Strømfjord. Teknisk rapport nr. 23. Grønlands Naturinstitut, 1999.

Lynge, F.: Kampen om de vilde dyr – en arktisk vinkel. Akademisk Forlag 1990, 147 pages.

Müller, R.: Vildtet og Jagten i Sydgrønland. 1906. 519 pages.

Oldendow, K.: Grønland – Folk og Land i vore Dage. Forlaget Fremad, København 1936, 214 pages.

Paldam, Martin: Grønlands økonomiske udvikling. Århus Universitetsforlag, 1994. 205 pages.

Pars, T.: Forbruget af traditionelle grønlandske fødevarer i Vestgrønland. Ph.D. afhandling, Det Sundhedsvidenskabelige Fakultet, Københavns Universitet, 2000. 124 pages.

Rydahl, K. & M.P. Heide-Jørgensen: Hvidbog om hvidhvaler. Rapport til fangerne i Grønland om den videnskabelige viden om hvidhvaler. Teknisk rapport nr. 35. Grønlands Naturinstitut, 2001.

Rydahl, K. & I. Egede (ed.): Seminar om de levende ressourcer. Teknisk rapport nr. 20. Grønlands Naturinstitut, 1998.

Salomonsen, F.: Fuglene på Grønland. Rhodos 1967. 343 pages.

Sejersen, F.: Myten om de bæredygtige inuit. Naturens Verden, nr. 5, årg. 83, 2000.

Siegstad, H. et al.: Grønlandske fisk, rejer, krabber og muslinger – en status iver vigtige ressourcer, 1. Oktober 1998. Teknisk rapport nr. 17. Grønlands Naturinstitut, 1998.

Links

www.atagu.ki.gl
Greenland's internet newspaper, established in 1995. Features comprehensive extracts of the most important community debates in Greenland, including issues such as hunting, environment and nature protection.

www.dpc.dk
The Danish Polar Center is an institution under the Research Ministry and its aim is to support and co-ordinate Danish polar research. Publishes the free-magazine 'Polarfronten' quarterly.

www.gh.gl
Greenland Home Rule Government.

www.greenland-guide.dk
Information about Greenland for the tourist. Hosted by Greenland Tourism Ltd.

www.inuit.org
Inuit Circumpolar Conference (ICC) is an international organisation representing 152,000 Inuit in the Arctic regions of Alaska, Canada, Greenland and Chukotka in Russia. ICC is aiming to strengthen the bond between the Inuit populations, strengthen their rights and interests as well as developing long-term strategies for the protection of the arctic environment.

www.knr.gl
Greenland Radio publishes daily the most essential news items from Greenland on this free online service.

www.natur.gl
Greenland Institute of Natural Resources, *Pinngortitaleriffik*, is the Greenland Home Rule's centre for wildlife research. The Institute collects knowledge regarding the current living resources in and around Greenland. This information is primarily used as the basis for the Institute's guidance to the Greenland Home Rule Government.

www.wwf.no/wwfap
WWF's Arctic program was established in 1992 for the advancement of nature protection in the Arctic.

Index